The Democratic Party Primary in Virginia
Tantamount to Election No Longer

Also published for the Institute of Government, University of Virginia:

Chester W. Bain, *Annexation in Virginia: The Use of the Judicial Process for Readjusting City-County Boundaries.* 1966. xiv, 258 pp.

Chester W. Bain, *"A Body Incorporate": The Evolution of City-County Separation in Virginia.* 1967. xii, 142 pp.

David G. Temple, *Merger Politics: Local Government Consolidation in Tidewater Virginia.* 1972. xii, 225 pp.

Thomas R. Morris, *The Virginia Supreme Court: An Institutional and Political Analysis.* 1975. xvi, 188 pp.

Weldon Cooper and Thomas R. Morris, *Virginia Government and Politics: Readings and Comments.* 1976. xviii, 438 pp.

The Democratic Party Primary
in Virginia
Tantamount to Election
No Longer

Larry Sabato

Published for
The Institute of Government, University of Virginia

University Press of Virginia
Charlottesville

THE UNIVERSITY PRESS OF VIRGINIA
Copyright © 1977 by the Rector and Visitors
of the University of Virginia

First published 1977

Library of Congress Cataloging in Publication Data

Sabato, Larry.
  The Democratic Party primary in Virginia.

  Bibliography: p. 157.
  Includes index.
  1. Primaries—Virginia—History. 2. Democratic Party. Virginia. I. Virginia.
University. Institute of Government. II. Title.
JK2075.V82S2   329'.0223'09755   77-9615
ISBN 0-8139-0726-8

Printed in the United States of America

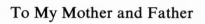

To My Mother and Father

Foreword

The Institute of Government is pleased to present this sixth volume in a continuing series dealing with various aspects of politics and public affairs in Virginia. This study of the Democratic primary helps to fill a major gap in our knowledge and understanding of politics in the Commonwealth. Given the essential role played by political parties in modern representative democracies, the way in which they nominate candidates deserves our careful attention. The nominating process in Virginia warrants consideration as well because it is distinctive in two important respects. By comparison with political parties in other American states, Virginia parties have unusual latitude in their nominating practices, and they have used that discretion to shift away from the heavy reliance on direct primaries characteristic of other states. By his examination of the origin and present status of the primary, the author greatly enhances our understanding of Virginia's political past and of its future prospects.

CLIFTON MCCLESKEY, Director
Institute of Government

Charlottesville, Virginia
April 1977

Preface

Each spring about this time, it seems, the question sprouts again: What has happened to the Democratic primary?

— James Latimer
Richmond *Times-Dispatch*
April 28, 1974

In Virginia, as in all of the one-party South, the Democratic primary election served for decades as more than a mere nominating process. The primary was clearly "tantamount to election" since the November general election inevitably ratified the Democratic primary choices. Not a single Virginia Democrat nominated for statewide office in the primary was defeated in the general election for more than threescore years after the primary's inception in 1905. The interest of the citizens naturally focused on the primary as the point of actual electoral decision, and voter participation in the primary sometimes even exceeded the turnout in the general election which followed.

In Virginia today, however, the Democratic primary has a position of greatly diminished importance. No contested statewide primary was held for six years after one in 1970, when only 2.1 percent of the voting age population cast a ballot. While the primary was renewed for the 1977 gubernatorial race, it is being used far less frequently on all electoral levels. As the Democratic primary completes its seventy-second year, the institution is clearly showing its age. The trend suggests that the Virginia primary may soon be placed—or may already be—in a state of semi-retirement.

How this drastic change came about is the subject of this study. The origin of the primary system in Virginia and in the nation is reviewed and analyzed in some detail. In many respects the Virginia experience with the primary has been unique. A progressive spirit of participatory democracy spread the primary throughout the United States in but a decade with hopes of eradicating "boss rule." Yet in Virginia a political machine was instrumental in the establishment of the primary, which complemented a restricted suffrage to give the state more than sixty years of virtually uninterrupted machine hegemony. The story of the primary's modern decline is as instructive as its rise. Many interrelated factors contributed to the simultaneous decline of machine and primary, and this process is also examined in this study.

The future of the primary system in Virginia is discussed in a final chapter, and considerable attention is given to a comparative evaluation of several methods of nomination. Special emphasis was placed on this evaluation since, for any political party and for the electoral system as a whole, the choice of the nominating process is as crucial as the general election result. Moreover, each nominating process may favor some aspirants to the detriment of others, thus affecting the kind and quality of public officials who are produced by the electoral system. It is my contention that, despite its past role and the partial responsibility for the decline of Democratic party fortunes which it bears, the primary election can have a legitimate place in the party's operation.

Throughout the text and tables, references are made to Virginia's regional areas, the urban corridor, and the congressional districts which existed at a particular time. For the reader's reference, a map of the Commonwealth's regions and urban corridor follows (fig. 1), and the various congressional district configurations from 1952 to the present are contained in Appendix I.

I wish to acknowledge and to thank Dr. Clifton McCleskey, director of the Institute of Government at the University of Virginia, who originally suggested the subject of my research and encouraged me throughout this undertaking. I share his conviction that more attention and concern should be focused on the nominating process at all levels of elective office. As they have in earlier projects, the staff of the Institute of Government proved indispensable. To Sandra Wilkinson, Angela Kelly, Dotti Slaughter, James Guinivan, and Janie Bowen, I express my appreciation once again. They deserve much of the credit for this book's publication, but any errors which remain are solely my responsibility.

LARRY SABATO

Oxford, England
March 1977

Figure 1. Virginia's Regional Areas and Urban Corridor

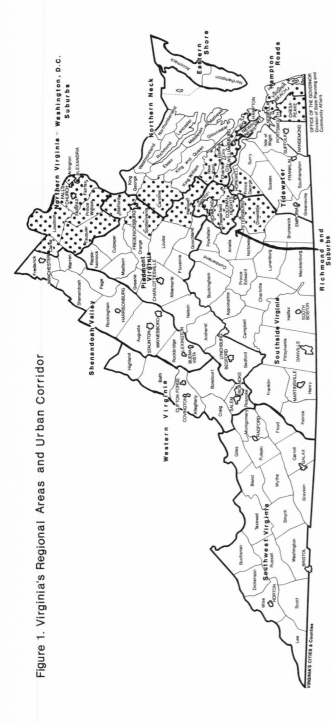

Cities and Counties in the Urban Corridor

NOTES: The base map was provided by the Division of State Planning and Community Affairs. The city and county boundaries are those as of November 1973. Changes have occurred in these boundaries after that date, but the outline of the urban corridor has remained intact.

Virginia's regional areas have no exactly defined boundaries. The groupings in this map are based upon descriptive accounts found in many reference works. See also Jean Gottmann, Virginia at Mid-Century (New York: Henry Holt and Company, 1955), pp. 143-226; and J. Harvie Wilkinson III, Harry Byrd and the Changing Face of Virginia Politics (Charlottesville: University Press of Virginia, 1968), p. 10.

The Hampton Roads area is an urban subset of the larger Tidewater regional area, and consists of the cities of Norfolk, Portsmouth, Virginia Beach, Chesapeake, Hampton, and Newport News.

Contents

Figures and Tables

Part I
Evolution of the Primary in Virginia and the Nation

Chapter 1

Origins of the Direct Primary
in the United States

IN 1897 the "high priest" of Progressivism, Robert M. LaFollette of Wisconsin, urged the adoption of the primary as an alternative to the convention system which then dominated the party nomination process.

Put aside the caucus and convention. They have been and will continue to be prostituted to the service of corrupt organization. They answer no purpose further than to give respectable form to political robbery. Abolish the caucus and the convention. Go back to the first principles of democracy; go back to the people. Substitute for both the caucus and the convention a primary election—held under the sanctions of law which prevail at the general elections—where the citizen may cast his vote directly to nominate the candidate of the party with which he affiliates and have it canvassed and returned just as he cast it. . . . Then every citizen will share equally in the nomination of the candidates of his party and attend primary elections as a privilege as well as a duty. It will no longer be necessary to create an artificial interest in the general election to induce voters to attend. Intelligent, well-considered judgment will be substituted for unthinking enthusiasm, the lamp of reason for the torchlight. The voter will not require to be persuaded that he has an interest in the election. He will know that he has. The nominations of the party will not be the result of "compromise" or impulse, or evil design—the "barrel" and the machine—but the candidates of the majority, honestly and fairly nominated.[1]

The relative of the convention and primary systems were heatedly debated by politicians and public alike, and in many elections throughout the country this debate became a key issue which often affected their outcome.[2]

The main argument for the primary was usually presented with great fervor, as LaFollette did: the bosses choose candidates in the convention while the people choose candidates in the primary. There can be little doubt that the movement for the primary in most states was an anti-

[1] Given Feb. 22, 1897, before the faculty and students of the University of Chicago, in a speech entitled, "The Menace of the Political Machine," excerpted from Robert M. LaFollette, *LaFollette's Autobiography* (Madison: University of Wisconsin Press, 1960), pp. 85–86.

[2] The Virginia gubernatorial elections of 1901 and 1905 and the election for U.S. Senate in 1905 all turned on the primary versus convention debate, as will be discussed in the following section. See the bibliography for many sources on the origin and growth of the direct primary system in the United States. See especially: Charles Merriam and Louise Overacker, *Primary Elections* (Chicago: University of Chicago Press, 1928).

machine endeavor. Proprimary politicians in many localities invariably invoked both the names of local party bosses and visions of convention corruption, which apparently was widespread. The primary, they consented, was less open to manipulation and political dealing. This more representative system supposedly would produce better candidates and more alert and aware voters.

Convention advocates believed they also had cogent arguments to support the retention of the more traditional nominating method. The convention, it was said, was more in harmony with our representative system of government. While the primary helped to destroy party organization, the convention helped to strengthen it. The deliberation and opportunity for compromise afforded by a convention produced a more unified party, in contrast to the often bitter primary factionalism. The nominating power and the platform-making belonged together, insisted convention advocates, who also suggested that their method was more efficient and less costly. Many admitted that serious abuses had occurred in conventions, but they thought these evils could be corrected with vigorous reforms of the convention process itself.

Whatever the merit of these arguments, the supporters of the primary won an almost complete victory within two decades of the start of the Progressive movement. It has been widely reported that the Progressives spawned the first primaries; yet operation of primary systems can be traced back to a much earlier period in the nation's history. According to one scholar, a form of the direct primary was provided for in the Hartford Constitution of 1638. After its introduction in Connecticut in 1689, it continued in use there until 1819.[3] Ironically, Connecticut was the last state to introduce the statewide primary in modern times, and since the adoption of their unique "challenge primary" law in 1955, the primary has been used only sparingly.

The direct primary was first used on local rather than state levels. The Democratic party of Crawford County, Pennsylvania, held a primary on September 9, 1842, thus rekindling the primary nomination system. The Democrats were reported to have abolished their convention in favor of the primary "as a means of restoring party harmony." Their experience, then, did not seem to support the argument made later by convention advocates that the convention fosters unity! Democrats ceased to use the primary in 1850, but the Republican party of Crawford County adopted it

[3] William Goodman, *The Two-Party System in the United States* (3d ed., New York: D. Van Nostrand Company, 1964), p. 127.

in 1860.[4] It is easy to understand why the primary was at first known as the Crawford County system.

Although the first recorded primary elections were held in northern states, the South adopted the primary system before any other region of the country.[5] Because of the one-party nature of the South, the party primary—which could provide a popular voice in the selection of the inevitable Democratic victor—found a natural home in Dixie. The primary, in turn, played a crucial role in promoting one-partyism in the South. In 1886 voters in Georgia elected pledged convention delegates in a primary and thereby determined the gubernatorial nomination in advance of the convention. During the 1870s several counties in Mississippi adopted the primary, and in 1902 the Mississippi legislature passed a primary law, though it did not have statewide application. In 1896 South Carolina had also passed a primary law for local application.

The West was also fertile ground for the primary proposal, "reflecting the Western dissatisfaction with formal political organization."[6] By the turn of the century, local primaries were widespread throughout the country, although almost all of them were optional and left to the discretion of local party committees. Some state legislatures did mandate required primaries for some cities and counties with significant and pervasive abuses in the convention system.

In 1902 LaFollette led his celebrated and successful fight for the adoption of the first statewide primary in Wisconsin, which was effective in 1903. The following year Oregon adopted a similar primary system, and other states took action in a rapid-fire reform sequence. By 1908 forty-seven states had enacted some type of primary legislation, although primaries were not held at regular intervals in all of these states. Fully thirty-one states provided statutorily for statewide primaries just five years after the Wisconsin primary law was adopted.[7] During this short period, as Charles Merriam has reported, there was a "gradual regulation by law of the affairs of what was originally regarded as a purely voluntary

[4] James W. Fesler, ed., *The 50 States and Their Local Governments* (New York: Knopf, 1967), p. 73; Goodman, p. 127.

[5] The basis for the discussion of Southern primary election history is Cortez A. M. Ewing, *Primary Elections in the South: A Study in Uniparty Politics,* (Norman: University of Oklahoma Press, 1953). See also Merriam and Overacker, and Goodman, pp. 127–28.

[6] Goodman, p. 128.

[7] For a description of the statutes and particulars of operation of each state's primary as of 1908, see Charles E. Merriam, *Primary Elections: A Study of the History and Tendencies of Primary Election Legislation* (Chicago: University of Chicago Press, 1909), pp. 273–88. Virginia's primary law at the time was considered "rudimentary" in comparison to those of other states.

association."[8] Optional primary laws became mandatory, local laws became statewide in focus, and primaries were converted from party operation to state operation.

The Virginia primary also began during the period of Progressive influence in the nation. While Progressive sentiments motivated some primary advocates in Virginia, the history of the primary's adoption and the effects which the primary had on state politics are unique to the Old Dominion. The origin of the direct primary in Virginia is examined in the next chapter.

[8] Ibid., p. 133.

Chapter 2

The Direct Primary Comes to Virginia

Although much of the generalized rhetoric found in histories of the Progressive movement is appropriate for the nation as a whole, it is wholly inadequate and even inaccurate as an explanation of the establishment of the direct primary in Virginia. One recent scholar noted:

As recently as the beginning of the 20th century the direct primary had come into use only in scattered communities in scattered states. For the first 110 years of the Republic the party caucus and then the party convention dominated the nominating of candidates for public office. Each gave way successively under the weight of criticism that they permitted, if not encouraged, the making of nominations by self-picked and irresponsible party elites. The history of the evolution of nominating methods in the United States above all is a story of the progressive triumph of the ethic and symbols of democracy.[1]

Actually, in Virginia the primary facilitated "the making of nominations by . . . party elites."

V. O. Key, Jr., noted that Virginia and North Carolina were the last southern states to establish the primary, and attributed this delay to the fairly keen two-party competition for statewide offices in the post-Reconstruction period.[2] In other words, demand for the primary was not as great in Virginia since some measure of meaningful popular control could be exercised in the general election; the Democratic party choice was not automatically elected in November. But the eventual establishment of full Democratic hegemony in Virginia does not provide a complete explanation for the adoption of the primary either.

The Martin Machine and Virginia's Primary

The triumph of the direct primary in Virginia owes much to the rise of Thomas Staples Martin and his Organization in the early 1890s. This may appear contradictory at first, since Martin proved to be a wily and erstwhile foe of the primary advocates. Yet it was Martin's acquiescence

[1] Frank J. Sorauf, *Party Politics in America* (Boston: Little, Brown and Company, 1968), p. 202.
[2] V. O. Key, Jr., *American State Politics: An Introduction* (New York: Knopf, 1956), p. 91.

which finally enabled the Democratic party to establish a direct primary in 1904. Not incidentally, the adoption of the primary system helped to ensure the survival and success of the Martin machine.

Thomas Staples Martin was an outstanding lawyer who represented the Chesapeake and Ohio railroad at a time when the rail industry was deeply involved in politics in Virginia and other states.[3] He managed the successful campaign of John Warwick Daniel for the U.S. Senate in 1885. The General Assembly elected the senators at that time, and Martin made many friends in the course of his endeavor for Daniel. In 1893 Martin himself announced for Virginia's other U.S. Senate seat. An unknown among the people of Virginia, Martin opposed the immensely popular Fitzhugh Lee, a former Confederate general who had just finished a term as governor. Railroad money funneled to General Assembly members as campaign contributions helped Martin to line up votes. There were also numerous promises of coveted committee assignments made by influential members of the Assembly supporting Martin to wavering or undecided legislators. When the election was held, Martin led Lee on every ballot and was elected on the sixth ballot. The election result was a shock to most Virginians, who had expected Lee to win easily. Martin's victory was widely denounced and gave many progressives pause on the method of election being employed.

The aftermath of the Martin election was felt at the 1897 state Democratic convention held in Roanoke. One of the leaders of the anti-Organization and progressive forces in Virginia, Congressman William A. Jones of Warsaw in Richmond County, tried to push the convention into adoption of the primary system of nomination. Fearful of losing his seat in 1899, Martin strongly opposed the Jones effort and used Senator Daniel, who was far more popular and influential with the delegates than he, to defeat the measure. Yet the close vote of 850 to 609 indicated substantial support for the primary among the party faithful. Martin was considerably frightened by the result, and he redoubled his reelection efforts and fortified his antiprimary strategy.[4]

---

[3] Virginius Dabney, *Virginia: The New Dominion* (New York: Doubleday and Company, 1971), p. 411. See also James A. Bear, Jr., "Thomas Staples Martin—A Study in Virginia Politics, 1883-1896" (M.A. thesis, University of Virginia, 1952).

[4] Ronald E. Shibley, "Election Laws and Electoral Practices in Virginia, 1867-1902: An Administrative and Political History" (Ph.D. diss., University of Virginia, 1972), pp. 195-98; Richard B. Doss, "John Warwick Daniel: A Study in the Virginia Democracy" (Ph.D. diss., University of Virginia, 1955).

The May Movement of 1899

In early spring 1899 state newspapers printed a call signed by fifty-two prominent Virginians for the convening of a meeting in May to discuss proposals for the popular election of U.S. senators.[5] Leaders of this "May Movement" included Congressman Jones, Attorney General Andrew Montague, Colonel Joseph E. Willard of Fairfax, John Goode of Bedford, William A. Anderson of Lexington, and former U.S. Senator Eppa Hunton.[6] When the meeting convened on May 10 in Richmond, 83 of 100 countries were represented and all cities but Danville and Petersburg had delegates. The total number of delegates exceeded 500. William Anderson was elected permanent chairman, and his election as well as comments from convention participants made it clear that the delegates were united in their intent to seek popular election of Virginia's U.S. senators.

Congressman Jones was enthusiastically received by the delegates, and he hinted at his own possible Senate candidacy opposing Martin later that year. There was some sentiment to "nominate" a candidate at the May meeting, but such an event did not materialize, to Jones's disappointment.[7] Nevertheless, it is no surprise that Martin viewed the meeting as a personal threat. As Virginius Dabney has wryly noted, Martin's "contention was not entirely without foundation."[8]

The delegates were at first divided on the proper method of party nomination of U.S. senators. Some favored a state convention, while others insisted on the primary. But, with the support of the leadership, the delegates unanimously adopted a resolution favoring the nomination by primary (for full text of the resolution, see Appendix II). The delegates also called for an amendment to the U.S. Constitution requiring direct election of U.S. senators rather than election by state legislature, and other states were invited to join Virginia in this effort. The delegates also recommended that the Democratic State Central Committee hold a primary (or convention if logistics required it for that year) to nominate a candidate for U.S. Senate in 1899—for the seat of Thomas S. Martin. The most directly anti-Martin statement in the resolution urged Democrats to refuse to nominate candidates for Assembly seats who would not pledge their full support both to the principles outlined in the resolution and to "a candidate [for the U.S. Senate] who is the open and

---

[5] Shibley.
[6] Norfolk *Virginian-Pilot*, May 8-11, 1899; Richmond *Times*, May 8-11, 1899.
[7] Shibley, p. 209.
[8] Dabney, *Virginia*, p. 428.

unequivocal advocate" of those same principles. Chairman Anderson was instructed to appoint an executive committee of twenty to carry out the work of a permanent "Democratic League for Reform in the Election of U.S. Senators."

Reaction to the aims of the conference was generally favorable. The *Virginian Pilot* commented editorially that the conference "did some good and great work, without committing any graver offense, as we think, than the impropriety of forgetting for a moment that it was in no sense an official body . . . represent[ing] the people of the State or the Democratic people or party of Virginia." This newspaper's editors endorsed the primary method of nomination even more strongly than the conference delegates, warning that "there is no gain in taking the Senatorial choice from the legislative representatives of the people and placing it in the hands of a convention. That is to take from the people what is pretended to be restored to them."[9]

Martin had been laboring diligently for his reelection since the Democratic state convention in 1897. After the May conference of 1899 disbanded he worked his will on the State Democratic Central Committee through its chairman, J. Taylor Ellyson. In an early meeting held on June 12 that caught Jones and his supporters by surprise, the central committee voted 37 to 11 to deny the requests of the May Movement. Ellyson also refused to give party campaign funds to state legislative candidates not pledged to Martin. Sensing the hopelessness of the battle, Congressman Jones decided not to run. Governor J. Hoge Tyler of Pulaski County did decide to oppose Martin, but he was not a particularly strong candidate and ran without the full support of the anti-Martin forces. Martin was overwhelmingly reelected in the next legislative session, where it was said he controlled 132 of 140 legislators. Tyler was not unaffected by his massive defeat, and in his next gubernatorial message to the General Assembly he strongly urged the direct election of U.S. senators and their nomination by primary.[10]

The Primary Gains Momentum

Gradually, however, the primary gained popular support in Virginia, as it did across the nation. Several localities were given permission by the General Assembly to hold primaries for local offices, including Portsmouth (1892), Norfolk (1894), Charlottesville (1898), and Prince William County

[9] May 14, 1899.
[10] Shibley, pp. 210–11; Dabney, *Virginia*, pp. 428–29.

(1900).[11] These local primaries were regulated almost totally by local party committees, as this excerpt from the law legalizing Prince William primaries indicates:

it shall be lawful for any political party in the county of Prince William previous to any general election held for the purpose of electing any federal, State, county, district, or corporation officers, to hold a primary election for the purpose of nominating candidates to be voted for in the said ensuing general election under such rules and regulations as may be prescribed by the local executive committee of such party: providing, however, that the expense of holding and conducting such primary election shall be borne by the party ordering the same.

The local committee of said party shall determine the rules and regulations under which the said primary election shall be held.[12]

The second sentence gave the local party the right to decide voting qualifications and to appoint all poll judges and clerks, although some local party committees allowed the candidates a voice in the latter's selections. Although the law required primary expenses to be borne by the party, the party committees assessed the candidates equally and they paid the bills. Virtually the only major state-ordered regulation in these early laws was a requirement, included in most of the laws permitting local primaries, that parties publish all primary regulations in newspapers or on posters a few days before the election.[13] Otherwise, the party had wide discretion—a precedent which would influence future primary legislation of statewide application in Virginia.

The General Assembly in 1900 yielded to the growing sentiment for popular election of U.S. senators and passed a joint resolution urging Virginia's two senators to support and work for such an amendment to the U.S. Constitution, the passage of which would have encouraged the establishment of the direct primary for Senate elections.[14] Martin proceeded to ignore the Assembly action, a fact which his eventual primary opponent in 1905 would not ignore. Any active opposition by Martin would have been quickly defeated and publicized by his many anti-Organization enemies. Moreover, although Martin could not have been gratified by the legislature's action in 1900, he had little reason to oppose

[11] Mary E. Pidgeon, ed., "Primary and Convention," *University of Virginia Record*, Extension Series, 10 (Nov. 1925): 20.

[12] Feb. 20, 1900, as amended April 2, 1902; see *Acts and Joint Resolutions of the General Assembly of the Commonwealth of Virginia, 1901-02* (hereafter referred to as *Acts of the Assembly*), c. 466, pp. 516-18.

[13] Pidgeon, p. 20.

[14] Allen W. Moger, *Virginia: Bourbonism to Byrd, 1870-1930* (Charlottesville: University Press of Virginia, 1968), p. 209.

the joint resolution strenuously. It had no force of law and merely allowed Assembly members to take the popular side of the issue.

The following year proved an unsettling one for Martin, and events were set in motion which would result in the eventual adoption of the primary system in Virginia. A man whose name reflected an unusual combination of Virginia bourbonism and Jacksonian populism was at the heart of the tumult in 1901—Andrew Jackson Montague, currently the state's attorney general and a leader of the anti-Organization forces.[15] Montague was an imposing and popular figure, and he stumped the state in 1901 seeking the Democratic nomination for governor. His main issue was the need for the direct primary to nominate both the governor and U.S. senators. His quest for pledged convention delegates was so successful that when the Democratic state convention met in Norfolk, the anti-Organization forces were clearly in control. Montague easily defeated Claude Swanson, Martin's candidate for governor, and Montague's associate, Joseph Willard, was nominated for lieutenant governor. More importantly from the proprimary perspective, Congressman William Jones was appointed chairman of the convention's resolutions committee. There was little surprise, then, when Jones's committee recommended that the party's state central committee be directed and empowered to draft and promulgate a plan for primary nominations. The tentative party plan, drawn up by the state central committee in response to the convention's directive, required primary elections for all Democratic candidates for statewide office, to be conducted under the general laws governing elections.[16] Candidates would bear all primary expenses, and whenever only one candidate filed for a particular office, the state or district party committee would declare the candidate to be the official party nominee. Interestingly, voting was to be viva voce, a provision strongly favored by Montague and Jones, who believed the Organization could more easily manipulate written ballots. This provision was dropped in favor of the secret ballot before the plan went into effect three years later. Reaction to the primary plan within and without the Democratic party was generally favorable, although considerable concern was expressed about burdening the candidates with the primary expenses.[17]

[15] See William Edward Larsen, "Governor Andrew Jackson Montague of Virginia, 1862–1937: The Making of a Southern Progressive" (Ph.D. diss., University of Virginia, 1961), condensed and published as *Montague of Virginia: The Making of a Southern Progressive* (Baton Rouge: Louisiana State University Press, 1965).

[16] Provisions of the primary plan are described in Moger, p. 204.

[17] Richmond *Times-Dispatch*, Aug. 23, Dec. 7, 10, 1902, and Jan. 11, 1903; Richmond *News-Leader*, April 9, 1903, and June 9, 10, 1904; see Moger, p. 204.

The actual implementation of this plan would not occur until 1905, and the particulars would have to be approved at the 1904 state convention. Montague and his supporters worried with considerable justification that Martin and his Organization would make attempts to debilitate or even kill the primary plan before it came into use. Martin had ample time and opportunity to do just that, but an important event in Virginia's history interceded which changed the very shape and character of Virginia politics.

A New Constitution and a Reconstituted Electorate

The Constitutional Convention of 1901–2, which designed and promulgated a new constitution for the Commonwealth, made the primary considerably more palatable for the Organization. As Robert K. Gooch has asserted, "The frank concern of the members of the [Constitutional Convention] was primarily to establish on a legal basis the disfranchisement of Negroes which had already been effected by the questionable means [of fraud, corruption, and quasi-legal barriers]." The convention established temporary voting registration regulations which required a prospective voter to explain any section of the new Constitution, unless he had paid property taxes to the state of at least one dollar or was a Confederate or Union veteran or the son of one. Local boards of registration "were given sweeping authority to decide whether the applicant's explanation was 'reasonable.' "[18]

The permanent voting registration impediments which were adopted were even more restrictive. A poll tax was required for all those who registered in 1904 or thereafter. A tax of $1.50 was to be paid for three preceding years, at least six months before the general election, to earn the right to cast a ballot. A person requesting registration was also required to apply "in his own hand-writing, without aid," and to "answer on oath any and all questions affecting his qualifications as an elector, submitted to him by the officers of registration." There is little doubt that these measures were widely abused. As Gooch reported: "The fundamental defect of the present registration system in Virginia is the discretionary authority which is vested in registration officials. . . .

[18] Robert Kent Gooch, *The Poll Tax in Virginia Suffrage History: A Premature Proposal for Reform (1941)* (Charlottesville: Institute of Government, University of Virginia, 1969), pp. 3–4; Dabney, *Virginia*, pp. 436–37. For a detailed account of the proceedings of the Constitutional Convention of 1901–2, see Ralph Clipman McDanel, *The Virginia Constitutional Convention of 1901–1902* (Baltimore: Johns Hopkins Press, 1928).

Abuse of the legal registration system at the hands of individual registrars takes the form of what is substantially arbitrary refusal on the part of a registrar to allow certain citizens to vote. . . . Some frank registrars readily admit that they ask questions [to prospective voters they do not wish to register] the answers to which they themselves do not know." [19] In adopting these restrictions, the convention broke the pledges of both the Democratic party and the General Assembly by not providing that their work be ratified in a general referendum. The convention delegates feared rejection of the new Constitution and its voting restrictions, especially since the electorate in a constitutional referendum would include the people who were to be disfranchised. [20]

The effect of these new voting restrictions can be easily gauged from an examination of the total presidential vote in the elections of 1900 and 1904. In the 1900 contest 264,240 votes were cast in Virginia, while four years later only 135,867 votes were recorded—a decrease of 48.6 percent! Not only did the new Constitution reduce the black vote, but many poor white voters, especially in Southwest Virginia, were also disfranchised. Virginius Dabney notes that 50 percent of Negro males over twenty-one years of age were illiterate, compared to only 12 percent of adult white males. In the Southwest, however, 24 percent of the adult white male population was illiterate. [21] .

In one of the great ironies of Virginia political history, the 1901–2 Constitutional Convention was controlled by anti-Organization Democrats. Yet they failed to see that a restricted electorate was a tailor-made situation for the Organization, creating as it did a smaller, more congenial, more homogeneous voting population which would be much easier to control. Not only did the new Constitution eliminate the black voter, a potential source of strength to the anti-Organization faction, but many white Republicans were also disfranchised. Allen W. Moger concluded that after the adoption of the 1902 Constitution, the Republican party "ceased to be a serious threat in Virginia, except in the ninth congressional district of the Southwest. Frequently divided into factions, for years it existed primarily in order to profit from patronage distributed by the national Republican administrations." [22]

Martin and his supporters were no quicker to recognize the real significance of the new Constitution than the leaders of the anti-Organization faction. The Organization continued to oppose the primary as a threat to

[19] Dabney, *Virginia*, pp. 436–47; Gooch, pp. 26–27.
[20] Dabney, *Virginia*, pp. 439–41.
[21] Ibid., p. 437.
[22] Moger, p. 203.

its control of the party. Conventions were thought much preferable to primaries, even though the Martin forces had lost control of two major conventions in recent years. Governor Montague, who hoped to challenge Martin for his Senate seat in a 1905 primary, correctly perceived Martin's continued opposition and feared that the Organization "could emasculate [the primary] with changes which would make it unpopular with the people [and then] at the next state convention would abolish what was thus far only an institution created and controlled by the Democratic party."[23]

Montague therefore attempted to secure mandatory primary legislation from the General Assembly in 1902 and 1903, but the Martin-controlled legislature balked. One bill, which had Montague's strong support, would have legalized the primary and had expenses paid by the counties and cities where the primary was held. Another bill, which Montague opposed, provided for a primary to elect state convention delegates, with the nominating power still resting with the convention. Finally, a frustrated Montague tried to influence the 1903 General Assembly elections to elect proprimary candidates. But his efforts (mainly restricted to correspondence) were not successful.

Yet even some Organization legislators were beginning to be impressed with the widespread support among the populace for the primary. Major newspapers in the state also strongly urged adoption of the system. And the Democratic party was still officially scheduled to convert to the primary method of nomination in 1905. All of these factors combined to lead to the passage of a primary bill in the 1904 General Assembly, a bill which was then defeated by the parliamentary maneuvers of Martin supporters. Moger described the situation and its results:

A Montague supporter, freshman Senator Lewis R. Machen of Alexandria, introduced a bill to legalize the [primary]. Both the Senate and the House passed the bill, the House with some amendments which would keep the selection of election judges in the hands of the county and city Democratic committees. During the last two days of the legislature two Martin men, Senators W. P. Barksdale and F. S. Tavenner, talked the bill to death and forced the Senate to adjourn without taking action. A charge by the Washington *Post* that the bill's defeat was a "coup of the Martin men" provoked a series of editorials in the Richmond *News Leader*. The paper believed the will of the people had been defeated by parliamentary tactics; "if Senator Martin is responsible . . . if he suggested, connived, or aided it or permitted it to be done . . . he has made [the issue] between Martin and the primary . . . between the machine and the people." Pointing out that the *News Leader* had been neutral in the pending

---

[23] Ibid., p. 204. Discussion of primary events before the 1904 state convention is taken primarily from Moger, pp. 204-6.

contest for the Senate between Martin and Montague, the paper promised a fight to the end against Martin if he opposed the primary. Martin denied any knowledge of the defeat of the Machen bill and said that the manner of nomination by Virginia Democrats was a matter of indifference to him, that he was willing to take his chances with any method. Though Barksdale also denied that he had ever talked to Martin about the Machen bill, the *News Leader* still held that "Barksdale was acting for what he believed to be the interests and supposed to be wishes of Senator Martin. . . . Senator Martin cannot avoid responsibility for the words and actions of his most enthusiastic supporters and representatives." Only after Martin, in an interview with the Washington *Post,* described himself as a friend of the primary and again denied that he was in any way responsible for the defeat of the Machen bill did the *News Leader* resume its position of neutrality in the senatorial contest. Montague was still dubious of Martin's innocence.[24]

The 1904 State Democratic Convention

Thus was Senator Martin drawn, somewhat unwillingly, to public support of the primary. Yet Montague still feared that Martin might derail the primary or postpone it until after his 1905 reelection. To forestall this eventuality, the Montague forces attempted to organize for 1904 as they had in 1901 to ensure a friendly majority at the state convention. They were successful in some areas, like Richmond, but were defeated by the well-organized machine in most places. Martin, who had been working feverishly since 1903, indisputably controlled a majority of the 1904 convention delegates.

Some delegates to the convention, including those from the cities of Richmond and Norfolk, were chosen in local primaries. Richmond also approved the primary plan by a vote of 1,909 to 194 in an early May referendum. Yet there was also considerable opposition to the establishment of state primaries from some Democrats who were not aligned with Senator Martin. These Democrats were primarily from the Southwest region. The *Bristol Courier* commented that "there is a strong sentiment in Bristol, Va., and in Southwest Virginia against the primary plan of nominating candidates in the Old Dominion, and when the State Convention meets in Richmond on [June 9], Bristol will be represented by a delegation that is opposed to making the primary plan general without regard to local conditions."[25]

[24] Ibid., p. 205. The quotes from the Richmond *News-Leader* are taken from the Jan. 26, Feb. 2, Mar. 14, 15, 21, and June 9, 1904, issues.

[25] *Bristol Courier*, June 2, 1904, as reported in the Richmond *Times-Dispatch*, June 4, 1904.

The desire of Southwest Virginians to retain their traditional convention deserves further comment, since opposition to the primary in the Southwest has remained alive to the present day. An examination of the Southwest's position in 1904 may also yield clues to the reasons for modern-day disenchantment with the primary in virtually all regions of Virginia.

Perhaps more than any other area of Virginia, the Southwest is unique culturally, economically, and politically. As Jean Gottmann has described it: "The southwestern tip of the commonwealth . . . encloses a triangle of great originality. . . . A very special mode of life has thus evolved." [26] The Southwest, then as now, was one of the poorest, least urban, unbourbon, and most Republican areas of Virginia. This last characteristic—Republicanism—is particularly important in explaining the distaste for the primary among Democrats of the region. A hardy and competitive brand of two-party politics survived even the shenanigans of the 1901–2 Constitutional Convention, and the many vicious, corrupt, wild, and woolly election battles in the Southwest Ninth Congressional District earned it the name of the "Fightin' Ninth." This tradition of strong politics led to many recorded instances of duels, feuds, and shootings at the polls—even between candidates. Politics was taken more seriously and conducted more intensely in the Southwest than in any other region of Virginia; this characteristic, too, persists in our time. The GOP was strong there, and Democrats believed that a convention helped them to marshal their troops with a minimum of dissension and in-fighting, or at least to settle any disputes out of public view. By contrast, the primary was held to intensify passions and to put those passions on display for the entire voting populace to see. Other parts of Virginia, especially after the 1902 Constitution became effective, could afford to fight it out publicly in a primary. There the well-publicized charges and countercharges which attended the primary battle could do little damage to the Democratic nominee, since there was an exceedingly small chance of most areas voting Republican. Even if the election had been bitter, Democrats who had supported the opposition would, at worst, "go fishing" on election day in November. In most regions of the Old Dominion, voting Republican was considered socially reprehensible if not an actual sin. But this was not so in the Southwest. Casting a Republican ballot was fairly commonplace and legitimate. Charges made in a primary could be used by the GOP to its great advantage in the general election. Supporters of the losing primary candidates had a legitimate alternative in November.

---

[26] Jean Gottmann, *Virginia at Mid-Century* (New York: Henry Holt, 1955), pp. 221–22.

Earlier it was suggested that the direct primary appealed to the South as a device for ensuring popular control in a one-party system. The two-party Southwest had no similar need for the primary; a choice was available in the general election. Indeed, the degree of two-party competition is the key to the fortunes of the primary in the Southwest and in all of Virginia's regions.[27] This will become clearer when the reasons for the decline of the primary are discussed in a later chapter.

Although the 1904 convention did establish mandatory primaries for statewide office, the delegates yielded to pressure from the Southwest and left the method of nomination at the congressional district and local levels to the discretion of the local and district party committees. This "local option" provision has remained a part of the Democratic party plan throughout the seventy years of the primary's existence, and Southwest Virginia has fully exercised it. Not a single congressional primary has been held there, and almost all other local nominations have been made by conventions. Several other areas of the state which joined the Southwest in 1904 in opposition to the primary—many Shenandoah Valley localities and some counties and cities in the Southside which are geographically close to the Southwest—also have frequently employed the convention method of nomination.[28]

To reiterate, the 1904 convention easily passed the statewide primary plan.[29] An alternative to the primary was proposed at the convention, which had been suggested by the Democratic State Central Committee as well when it refused the primary in 1899. Basically, the proposal suggested that the people in each legislative district instruct their assemblyman on their choice for U.S. senator by means of a primary. This choice would not be binding on the legislator, however. Proposed by a state senator, it was "an old familiar friend of members of the General Assembly" since it had been introduced unsuccessfully in the legislature in 1903.[30] Although sup-

---

[27] In attempting to explain the Southwest's affinity for conventions a less grand but no less valid reason should not be ignored. Politics was very much of a social affair in the Southwest and appeared to play a significant role in the organization of the social system of this region. The spirit of a convention—the whooping, the hollering, and the speechmaking—seems to fit the spirit of the Southwest very well. The primary election, while perhaps providing for a broader participation, did not include mechanisms which could capture this same spirit of camaraderie and good times.

[28] Henry County, which is located in Southside but is close to the Southwest, was particularly vociferous in its opposition to the primary. For several years after the adoption of the statewide primary, Henry County Democrats would regularly instruct their delegates to party conclaves to attempt repeal of the primary provision.

[29] Accounts of the convention carried in the Richmond *Times-Dispatch* and the Norfolk *Virginian-Pilot*, June 8–12, 1904, are the sources of the discussion which follows.

U.S. Constitution with the power of senatorial election. But "as a matter of party rule and party honor," the Democratic nominee for U.S. Senate would be supported by the Democratic members of the General Assembly, although no member of the legislature, Democrat or Republican, was legally bound to do so.[3]

The election for U.S. Senate drew the greatest attention from public and politicians alike. Governor Andrew Montague filed to oppose Senator Martin and promised a vigorous five-month campaign. Montague's platform for his 1901 gubernatorial bid had been headed by his advocacy of primary elections, and the party primary again proved to be his main issue. He repeatedly attacked Martin for the senator's earlier opposition to the primary, and he painted Martin's machine in sinister hues as well. Martin in turn stressed his experience and considerable seniority and lambasted Montague for his "inaccurate charges." He suggested that not he but Montague was the master of a "political machine."[4]

The contest for the governorship was overshadowed by the Senate race, but there, too, the Democratic factions were joined in combat. Congressman Claude A. Swanson, who had unsuccessfully opposed Montague in 1901, was the Organization candidate for governor. He was opposed by Lieutenant Governor Joseph E. Willard, the anti-Organization candidate, and Judge William H. Mann.

Never before had the people of Virginia been treated to such a public display of political fireworks. The impact of the first primary was clearly great. The Richmond *Times-Dispatch* noted that "for the first time in many years candidates went before the people on the stump and made a close canvass of the entire State, thus seeing in person a large proportion of the 80,000 voters, who, it is expected, will participate in the primary. Naturally such a campaign . . . has developed into one of considerable feeling and bitterness and some excitement." As the Southwest Virginians had suspected, the primary offered a vast public forum for the airing of campaign charges and countercharges and a lengthy period in which to continue this display. "As fast as one charge was disposed of and abandoned, another was unearthed."[5]

[3] Richmond *Times-Dispatch*, July 19, 1905.

[4] Martin thus inaugurated a familiar theme which would be heard again and again in clear-cut Organization versus anti-Organization primary battles. Martin and his successor, Harry Byrd, sought to depict their political Organizations as mere "associations of like-minded men." If a voter insisted on seeing a political machine in that, then he should realize that the anti-Organization faction had its "machine" as well. The primary, then, simply pitted one machine against the other—or so the Organization would have the voter believe.

[5] Aug. 20, 1905.

If the election results are any guide, Senator Martin had the better of the campaign debate. He easily defeated Montague, securing 56.3 percent of the vote. The incumbent senator carried all ten congressional districts and two-thirds of all cities and counties. Claude Swanson did almost as well in a three-way race, garnering 51.2 percent of the vote in the gubernatorial contest. The Organization candidate for lieutenant governor, J. Taylor Ellyson, who also served as chairman of the Democratic party, was overwhelmingly elected with 79.2 percent. The incumbent attorney general, William A. Anderson, was also easily reelected with 61.4 percent of the vote. Anderson, a nominal anti-Organization man, had wisely remained neutral in the Martin-Montague contest. (For an accounting of the results of all Virginia primary elections for governor, lieutenant governor, and attorney general from 1905 to 1973, see Appendix III. Similar data for U.S. Senate primaries are compiled in Appendix IV.)

The Organization's hopes for the primary system were thus fulfilled. Its gamble that a restricted electorate would be a manageable electorate proved accurate and fortuitous. Allen Moger commented that "a small electorate and thorough organization by Hal Flood [Martin's campaign manager and Harry Byrd's uncle] were important in explaining Martin's victory. In every county the Martin forces had control of the election machinery and were carefully organized around the traditional office-holders and party workers, while less than half the state's precincts had a Montague organization. . . . The politically ambitious love a winner, and the signs in 1905 pointed to Martin rather than to Montague. Few of the politically prominent would actively support the governor."[6]

The Machine Benefits

The primary paid many dividends to Martin. Before the 1905 election Martin's image had been one of the political boss controlled by special interest groups like the railroads. He was a favorite target not only of the anti-Organization Democrats but also of major newspapers throughout the state.[7] But Martin's victory gave them pause and added tremendous legitimacy and stature to the much maligned senator. The *Times-Dispatch* admitted that "Senator Martin stands forth as the clear, square and incontestable choice of the Democrats of Virginia," and even the *Virginian-*

[6] Moger, p. 211.
[7] The Norfolk *Virginian-Pilot* was particularly emphatic in its editorial denunciations of Martin.

Pilot concurred with that appraisal.[8] Martin may have foreseen the additional benefits which would accrue to him from the primary when he agreed to the adoption of the system in 1904. In any event, whatever fears or resentment he harbored against the primary must surely have evaporated after his victory.

Accordingly, the primary as a method of nomination was heaped with praise from Organization stalwarts as well as the traditionally antimachine press. "Advocates of the primary . . . will probably take encouragement from the result of this first trial of the system. The campaign was enlightening. The people of Virginia, the men who will support the ticket named yesterday, learned a vast deal about those who appealed for their suffrages. . . . Candidate and voter met face to face. The meeting could but have been helpful to both, especially to the successful candidate in giving him intimate knowledge of the people whom he is to serve." One newspaper editorialized a widely agreed upon conclusion to the 1905 election. "The primary has been justified from every point of view and should now be regarded as an established institution in Virginia."[9]

Some disagreement remained on particulars of Virginia's primary system, however. Considerable concern was voiced about the method of financing the primaries. As discussed earlier, the political party had the ultimate financial responsibility for holding primaries, and the party passed the bill to all candidates. In 1905, for instance, the Democratic State Central Committee assessed all candidates as follows: U.S. senator and governor, $1,500 each; lieutenant governor, $100; attorney general, $500; treasurer, $350; secretary of the commonwealth, commissioner of agriculture, and superintendent of public instruction, $200 each. About $9,600 was expected to be raised in assessments by the Democratic party.[10] Many in the party and the press contended that the state should absorb primary expenses for statewide contests, with cities and counties paying the bills for local primaries. The ultimate resolution of this debate over financing and of similar disputes about other aspects of the primary's operation would have to await the adoption of a statewide primary law.

One interesting aspect of the 1905 primary was the orderly way in which it was conducted despite the hard-fought contests taking place. The comparison with recent conventions was inevitable. In the 1901 state Democratic convention and the local gatherings leading up to it, there were "fist fights, riots, pistol brandishings," and many other outbursts, while the 1905 primary "proved to be the most orderly election held

[8] Richmond *Times-Dispatch*, Aug. 24, 1905; Norfolk *Virginian-Pilot*, Aug. 25, 1905.
[9] Richmond *Times-Dispatch*, Aug. 23, 24, 1905.
[10] Moger, p. 208n.

in the state for years." Raymond Pulley has suggested that the system of nomination used before the adoption of the primary may have contributed to the raucousness attending party affairs at that time. Statewide candidates had been selected by a variety of methods. Governor, lieutenant governor, and all other state officers were nominated by conventions composed of delegates previously selected in hundreds of local conventions and "mass meetings." U.S. senators were elected by a party caucus in the General Assembly, while candidates for the Assembly were nominated by local primaries or conventions. "The great confusion in the nomination procedure actually encouraged a continuation of factionalism and political strife within the organization, but the uniform system introduced under the primary worked to promote harmony among the contending groups and personalities."[11]

The suffrage articles in the new Virginia Constitution were thought to have accomplished their purpose. The black vote in the 1905 primary was miniscule and inconsequential. Of the 147,000 blacks of voting age in 1900, about 21,000 were registered in late 1902; by 1905 fewer than half of this number were believed to have met the poll tax requirement.[12] The primary voters had become "a select electorate—a great party of white friends, animated . . . by the lofty purpose of getting the very best candidates possible."[13] With the restricted suffrage and curtailment of the Republican vote, the primary had now been established as the real point of electoral choice. This was precisely what the Constitutional Convention of 1901–2 had intended. As convention delegate William A. Anderson, future attorney general and strong primary advocate, commented in 1901: "If we can get an effective suffrage *article* in the new Constitution, the *primaries* will or can be made to be the real elections."[14]

Delusions of Progressivism

As the story of the origin of Virginia's primary is concluded, one cannot help but dwell on a recurrent historical error which pervades much of the scholarly literature on the Progressive movement. The direct primary has been consistently referred to as a democratic innovation of Progressivism, and visions of Robert LaFollette are inevitably conjured up by scholars

---

[11] Raymond H. Pulley, *Old Virginia Restored: An Interpretation of the Progressive Impulse, 1870–1930* (Charlottesville: University Press of Virginia, 1968), pp. 126, 128.

[12] Dabney, *Virginia,* pp. 446.

[13] Richmond *Dispatch,* April 18, 1899.

[14] Anderson to John C. Parker, June 30, 1901, quoted in Pulley, p. 128.

making too hasty a generalization. For example, Thomas D. Clark and Albert D. Kirwan concluded that the primary in the South "broadened the base of the election process, bringing the mass of voters into the choice of candidates and freeing them from the domination of an oligarchy led by planters, bankers, railroad officials, and corporate executives."[15] Although this may have occurred in some southern states, the establishment and operation of Virginia's primary is clearly an exception.

While criticizing some authorities, it is only fair to note that not everyone has ignored the primary's potential attractiveness and usefulness to an efficient political machine, although this observation appears restricted to the contemporaries of the Progressive movement. Virginia's Richard E. Byrd, speaker of the House of Delegates and the prime author of Virginia's primary law, evaluated the primary system in 1921 by reflecting on the Old Dominion's experience:

Primary advocates believed that the primary is a better system for ascertaining the will of the people than the convention. Experience seems to have demonstrated that the contrary is true. The direct primary aids popular control in theory, but not in fact. A method of political control theoretically popular frequently destroys the fact of popular control.

In general people will only give a certain amount of attention to public affairs. When the machinery of a political system demands more attention than the people are willing to give, interested persons who have means to create and operate organizations take control and nominations are made by minorities.[16]

Even earlier in 1909 Henry Jones Ford, a prominent newspaper editor and Princeton professor, chided his Progressive associates.

One continually hears the declaration that the direct primary will take power away from the politicians and give it to the people. This is pure nonsense. Politics has been, is and always will be carried on by politicians, just as art is carried on by artists, engineering by engineers, business by business men. All that the direct primary, or any other political reform, can do is to affect the character of the politicians by altering the conditions that govern political activity, thus determining its extent and quality. The direct primary may take advantage and opportunity from one set of politicans and confer them upon another set, but politicians there will always be so long as there is politics.[17]

---

[15] Thomas D. Clark and Albert D. Kirwan, *The South since Appomattox: A Century of Regional Change* (New York: Oxford University Press, 1967), p. 112, quoted in Pulley, p. 129. Pulley quotes other Progressive authorities and includes an excellent analysis of the causes and effects of the primary system in Virgihia, pp. 127–31.

[16] Byrd to H. G. Peters, Mar. 8, 1921, reproduced in Pidgeon, p: 83.

[17] Austin Ranney, *The Doctrine of Responsible Party Government* (Urbana: University of Illinois Press, 1962), pp. 72–73.

The establishment of the primary and the results of the first such election in 1905, then, represented a major turning point in Virginia's political history. After many indecisive skirmishes with its more progressive foes, the traditionalist Organization had triumphed. The direct primary and the suffrage clauses of the new Constitution combined to forge a new political order for the Commonwealth—which was simply a more firmly entrenched version of the old political order. The anti-Organization faction of the Democratic party was not totally subjugated, of course. It was still capable of contesting elections and had some credible candidates and a measure of organizational and financial strength. Yet its candidates could scarcely hope to be cast as anything but decided underdogs in any contest with the far superior Organization forces. And the Republicans provided little additional competition. The Organization candidate Claude Swanson defeated the Republican gubernatorial nominee Judge L. L. Lewis in November 1905 by a vote of 83,544 (64.6 percent) to 45,795.[18] Virginia had truly become "almost a one-party system within a one-party system."[19]

[18] Moger, p. 214.

[19] V. O. Key, Jr., applied this description to Virginia under the Byrd Organization, but it seems to apply equally well to the state under Martin's aegis. See Key, *Southern Politics in State and Nation* (New York: Knopf, 1949), p. 18.

Chapter 4

The Primary and Machine Mature

Senator Daniel was renominated in 1907 without opposition, so the next test of the primary came in the gubernatorial battle of 1909. The Organization candidate was William Hodges Mann, vice-president of the Virginia Anti-Saloon League, which had been spearheading the drive for prohibition in the state. The Martin machine had accommodated Mann, who had been defeated by Organization candidate Swanson four years earlier, and Mann in turn accommodated Martin. At Martin's urging Mann renounced the goal of prohibition, although his new pledge was later partially retracted. Martin managed to turn out the "whiskey vote" for him despite the fact that Mann was opposed by an anti-Organization candidate, Harry St. George Tucker, who was much more acceptable to the "wets." Tucker strongly supported local option on prohibition, i.e., the right of each city or county to decide the issue for itself. The whiskey deals which Martin was able to conclude successfully on Mann's behalf indicate again that the newly restricted electorate was a more manageable one; deals could be enforced with much greater ease.[1]

Tucker was a popular figure, and the prohibition issue was undoubtedly beneficial to him in many areas. Yet Mann was able to produce a 53.5 percent victory with the aid of the Organization. Machine favorite J. Taylor Ellyson again overwhelmed his opponent with 69.1 percent of the vote to win reelection as lieutenant governor. Finally, another candidate acceptable to the Organization, Samuel W. Williams, was easily elected attorney general with 65.4 percent. Just four years earlier, Williams had been defeated for that office by William Anderson, who did not seek reelection in 1909. After Judge Lewis's trouncing in the governor's race in 1905, Republicans realized they had little chance of electoral success. The 1909 election only confirmed their worst fears, as Mann decisively defeated Republican William P. Kent in November. This result was not entirely displeasing to many in the GOP, since an unsuccessful party would be a smaller party. There would therefore be a greater

[1] See Moger, pp. 216–18.

portion of the spoils from national Republican administrations for themselves.[2]

The Independents Try Again

A series of defeats did not stop the anti-Organization forces from trying, however. A double U.S. Senate primary in 1911 provided yet another opportunity for victory. Senator Martin sought reelection, and the death of Senator Daniel left a vacancy to be filled. Congressman William A. Jones finally yielded to his senatorial ambitions and filed to oppose Martin. Governor Mann had appointed former governor and current congressman Claude Swanson to Daniel's seat after an internal Organization battle.[3] Swanson then filed for election for the remainder of Daniel's Senate term. Another anti-Organization stalwart, Congressman Carter Glass, opposed him in the primary.

It was a hard-fought and bitter election battle, and some corruption was alleged against Martin and Swanson. The anti-Organization candidates were not without their resources, either. In early March 1910 a Virginia Democratic League was formed to promote the cause of the insurgents. Leaders of the league included a past governor, Andrew Montague, and a future governor, John Garland Pollard. The direct primary theme could still be detected, as the league called for popular general election of U.S. senators and the incorporation of the primary system into state law with expenses borne by the public treasury. Primary candidates still paid all election costs in 1911. The Democratic State Central Committee assessed each Senate candidate $3,000, an unusually large assessment. But the committee explained that there were only a few candidates in 1911 and that the last statewide primary had cost $12,000.[4]

Not surprisingly, Martin and his machine partner won both elections, and the massive margins of their victories were impressive. In 1905 Martin won with 56.3 percent of the vote, but in 1911 he garnered 67.5 percent. Claude Swanson even bettered Martin's performance, securing an astounding 70.1 percent of the vote. It is little wonder that Swanson in 1916 and Martin in 1918 were granted new Senate terms without primary opposition. For the moment, at least, the anti-

---

[2] See J. Harvie Wilkinson III, *Harry Byrd and the Changing Face of Virginia Politics* (Charlottesville: University Press of Virginia, 1968), p. 199.

[3] Mann had wanted originally to appoint Congressman "Hal" Flood, Harry Byrd's uncle.

[4] Dabney, *Virginia*, pp. 456–57; Moger, pp. 222, 224n.

Organization forces were stunned and devastated. The irony, of course, was that Glass and Jones had personally helped to frame the 1902 Constitution, and Glass had been the author of the restrictive suffrage clause which played no small part in his humiliating defeat in 1911. Yet, even then, Organization victories were not universal. Jones and Glass both won reelection to the U.S. House of Representatives in 1912 Democratic primaries against strongly backed machine candidates.

A Primary Law for Virginia

Many ironies have been identified in the course of this accounting of the simultaneous establishment of primary and machine control. A final major irony presents itself in the enactment of the last plank in the anti-Organization's "primary platform" by the Organization itself in 1912. Richard Evelyn Byrd, father of Harry Byrd and then serving as speaker of the House of Delegates, introduced and guided to passage in the 1912 General Assembly a statewide primary bill which has since become known as the Byrd Law.[5] Until that year the state legislature had been notably unsuccessful in filling the mandate of section 36 of the 1902 Constitution, which provided that the Assembly should pass laws for "securing the regularity and purity" of primary elections.[6] As discussed earlier, maneuvers by Martin supporters defeated a primary law in the 1904 legislative session, and no subsequent session seemed able or willing to pass one, perhaps content to leave the primary's particulars to party regulation.[7] It was eight years from the adoption of the primary to the successful passage of a law which regulated and firmly implanted it in the election machinery. Perhaps these years can be regarded as a testing period for the primary, ending in 1912 when tentative support became permanent as the system became a part of the state's statutory superstructure.

As passed and signed by Governor Mann (who had recommended a similar bill) in March 1912, and amended in 1914, the Byrd Law provided for a uniform primary day across the state, set for the first Tuesday in August. Ballot boxes and printing of ballots would be supervised by local boards of election rather than party officials. A plurality of the vote

[5] Discussion of the bill's provisions in the following paragraphs is derived from *Acts of the Assembly, 1912*, c. 307, pp. 611–19, and *Acts of the Assembly, 1914*, c. 305, pp. 513–25.

[6] Pidgeon, p. 21.

[7] The only statute which concerned the primary appears to be one stating that all laws "intended to secure the purity of general elections" should, as far as possible, be applied to primaries. See ibid., p. 21.

would be sufficient to nominate a party candidate; there was no provision for a runoff election if a candidate failed to secure a majority. (Most southern states did allow for a runoff, and the reasons for Virginia's exception will be developed later in this study.) If more than one party chose to hold a primary, a voter would have to declare his party choice and select only one party's ballot at the polling place; he could not vote for candidates of both parties. This is a form of the "closed primary," which forty-three states had as of 1968.[8] Some of the states require the declaration of party affiliation at the time of registration; but most, like Virginia, do not truly have a closed primary, since without party registration or a similar device, there is no effective way of establishing party membership. Each party would be allowed to appoint election judges to conduct the primary for that party. No person could vote in a party's primary unless he had voted for the party's candidate at the last general election. This "loyalty" provision would prove to be a most troublesome and controversial section in years to follow.[9] Further, any voter could be challenged on loyalty to his party at the polls by any other voter or official. If challenged, the voter was required to swear to one of the party's primary judges that he fulfilled his party requirements. The ballots and the official election returns were to be the charge of the secretary of the Commonwealth and a new state board of canvassers. Previously, the party chairman had been ceded this responsibility.

Candidates received considerable new benefits and protection in provisions of the Byrd Law. No longer would the candidates have to bear the costs of holding primaries. The state assumed all expenses for statewide primaries and required cities and counties to pay the bills for local primaries held within their jurisdictions. However, each primary candidate had to pay a candidacy filing fee equal to 2 percent of the annual salary of the office for which he was running.[10] This fee was considerably less

[8] Sorauf, *Party Politics in America*, p. 204.

[9] As written in statute and summarized here, it appears reasonable that an individual attempting to vote in, say, the 1917 Democratic governor's primary would have had to have voted for the Democratic slate of presidential electors in November 1916. As we shall see shortly, however, an attorney general in 1929 would reach a very different conclusion, perhaps because of more ambiguous language added in 1924.

[10] The General Assembly passed an amendment to the Byrd Law on Feb. 12, 1918, which provided that all filing fees should be kept in a separate and distinct account, rather than being directly deposited in the state's general fund. Each year all money contained in the "primary fee fund" was paid to the state's Literary Fund. Many candidates through the years have not been able to resist the claim that they contributed to quality education for the citizenry even before they were elected. See *Acts of the Assembly, 1918*, c. 40, pp. 96–97.

than most of the assessments which party officials had been making for primary expenditures. Each candidate would also be required to file a written declaration of candidacy and a certain number of signatures of qualified voters from his district or the state with party officials, not less than sixty days before the primary. The contesting of an election was declared to be the candidate's right, and would be conducted by specified courts. Previously, the party's chairman and executive committee heard disputes, a situation that was far more likely to involve purely political factors in the settlement of election grievances.

The Byrd primary law never specifically mentioned the Democratic party. Rather, the primary method of nomination at public expense was made optional for all parties which had received at least 25 percent of the vote in the last presidential election. A Democratic member of the state Senate was moved to comment that "a genuine primary law takes no recognition of the Democratic party or of the Republican party, but addresses itself to the good of the people as a whole, regardless of party."[11] Despite this display of nonpartisanship, the state GOP showed no interest in the primary either before or after the enactment of the Byrd Law, until 1947. As we shall see, the results of the Republican primaries held in that year and in 1949 reveal some of the reasons for the Virginia GOP's adherence to the convention method.

Several unsuccessful efforts to amend the Byrd Law deserve mention.[12] In 1914 the Organization governor, Henry C. Stuart, proposed an interesting voting arrangement for the primary whereby voters would be allowed to indicate on their ballots a first and second choice for each office which had more than two candidates. The General Assembly found his suggestion novel but unconvincing. An attempt was made in 1912 to provide statutorily for compulsory primaries for all statewide offices (thus removing the party's option), but the amendment received the votes of only four senators.[13] Two years later the amendment's supporters made yet another try to secure the compulsory provision, and even arranged for three-time Democratic presidential nominee William Jennings Bryan to address the Assembly on behalf of the amendment. But the legislature again defeated the clause. Despite this failure to adopt a compulsory provision, the passage of the Byrd Law indicated that the primary was now firmly set in both the mechanism and mentality of the Democratic party.

[11] Pidgeon, p. 20.
[12] Ibid., pp. 21–28.
[13] One of those senators was G. Walter Mapp, of the Eastern Shore, who would later oppose Harry F. Byrd, Sr., in the 1925 gubernatorial primary—a primary which rumors had suggested the Organization would cancel in favor of a convention.

The same year as the original Byrd primary law was passed, the Seventeenth Amendment to the U.S. Constitution establishing popular election of U.S. senators in the November election was ratified. The Congressional Research Service has concluded that "the ratification of this Amendment was the outcome of increasing popular dissatisfaction with the operation of the originally established method of electing senators." Deadlocks had occurred in some legislatures, leaving seats vacant for long periods, and the turmoil caused by the selections had forced many state legislators to neglect their other duties. Citizens throughout the country also were repulsed by the shenanigans of corrupt political organizations and special interests in choosing members of Congress's upper house. The Seventeenth Amendment did not bring any radical change to Virginia or the nation. By 1912 twenty-nine states, including, of course, the Old Dominion, were nominating senators on a popular basis. Legislatures in most states still had the legal power of final choice, but in fact they were relegated to a position comparable to that of presidential electors, as was the case in Virginia. At least two states actually required by law that all legislative candidates had to agree to support the senatorial candidate polling the most votes in the primary.[14] The Seventeenth Amendment thus brought to a close the two-decade Progressive battle for popular election of U.S. senators.

More Political Maneuvers

The first unopposed gubernatorial candidate in a Democratic primary in Virginia ran in 1913. Henry Carter Stuart of the Southwest accomplished this feat, which was to be repeated only once more.[15] Stuart was of an independent mind, but he was popular and had run Bascom Slemp, Virginia's GOP leader and only congressman, a close though losing race earlier. As the organizations of both Martin and Byrd sometimes found it necessary to do, Stuart was allowed to run unopposed in 1913. Through this accommodation process Stuart was also "absorbed" by the Organization, and his relations with the machine's leaders were harmonious throughout his term.[16] There were contests for the other state offices

[14] Congressional Research Service, Library of Congress, *The Constitution of the United States of America: Analysis and Interpretation* (Washington, D.C.: U.S. Government Printing Office, 1973), pp. 1565–66.

[15] Mills E. Godwin ran unopposed in the 1965 primary for governor. There was also no primary contest in 1973 for governor because no candidate filed. The candidate in the one Republican primary for governor in 1949 was also unopposed.

[16] Dabney, *Virginia,* p. 463.

in the 1913 primary, however. Two-term incumbent J. Taylor Ellyson once again won the lieutenant governor's post, although with a reduced majority. In 1905 he had won 79.2 percent of the vote; in 1909 he garnered 69.1 percent; but in 1913 Ellyson finished with only 61.2 percent of the vote.[17] The incumbent attorney general, Samuel W. Williams, was actually defeated for renomination by a narrow margin. John Garland Pollard, who had been associated with the anti-Organization faction, scored a plurality victory of 47.0 percent to 45.4 percent for Williams. Ellyson's poor showing and Williams's defeat suggest that the Organization may have been caught napping, lulled by not having to do battle over the gubernatorial post.

Four years later the Organization was not napping but was defeated nonetheless. A three-way race developed for governor in 1917 which was complicated immensely by the prohibition issue. Lieutenant Governor Ellyson was the Organization candidate, supported by both Martin and Bishop James Cannon, Jr., powerful leader of the prohibition forces. Ellyson was "dry" for political purposes, although it was no secret that he was rather "wet" personally. Attorney General John Garland Pollard was also "dry," and he was supported by some prohibition supporters as well as anti-Organization leaders including Carter Glass. The only "wet" in the race was Westmoreland Davis, a political unknown who was associated with no Democratic faction, although he began to attack the machine vigorously during the campaign. Davis was a total abstainer personally, but he strongly opposed the views and tactics of Bishop Cannon.[18]

This election proved to be confusing for the voters and uncontrollable for the machine. A split in the "dry" vote resulted in the plurality election of the first Organization opponent on a statewide level since the adoption of the primary system. Although Westmoreland Davis only won 43.9 percent of the vote, he carried seven of ten congressional districts and carried every important city in the state except Roanoke, Danville, and Bristol.[19] Newspapers and commentators in Virginia and across the nation pointed to Davis's victory as a repudiation of the Martin machine and a sign that the Organization was falling apart. It was nothing

[17] Although the 1913 election for lieutenant governor was technically a three-way race, one of the candidates, Alexander J. Wedderburn, withdrew before the election but too late to have his name removed from the ballot. Still, Wedderburn drew only 2.4 percent of the vote. For more information on this election, see Appendix III, note a.

[18] See Virginius Dabney, *Dry Messiah: The Life of Bishop Cannon* (New York: Knopf, 1949); Jack Temple Kirby, *Westmoreland Davis: Virginia Planter-Politician, 1859–1942* (Charlottesville: University Press of Virginia, 1968).

[19] Kirby, p. 70. J. Taylor Ellyson carried the three cities mentioned.

of the kind, of course, but rather was a product of the unique political situation brought about by prohibition.[20] An example to support this contention can be found in Norfolk which at that time was an Organization stronghold. But Norfolk was also very "wet," and the Democratic Organization there broke with Martin's prohibitionist candidate to give Davis a landslide. In this same election, though, the machine kept control of the General Assembly delegation in Norfolk and throughout the state. Organization-tilting John R. Saunders was elected attorney general with 53.8 percent of the vote. Clearly, then, the Davis election was an aberration. A restricted electorate and the primary system virtually assured the resurgence of the machine.

The Machine Fights Back

That resurgence came about simultaneously with the changing of the Organization guard and the absorption of yet another independent challenger. In 1919 Senator Martin died after serving only a year of the term won in 1918. Governor Davis was presented with the unique opportunity to appoint an anti-Organization man to the Senate vacancy. After discussions with Congressman Carter Glass, Davis appointed the Lynchburg legislator to the seat.[21] According to Davis, he was given assurances by Glass of the latter's continuing opposition to the machine. The Organization, temporarily coordinated by Senator Claude Swanson and Congressman Hal Flood,went to work to woo Glass.[22] Flood placed Glass in nomination for the presidency at the 1920 Democratic national convention, and the Organization allowed a grateful Glass to run unopposed in 1920 for the Democratic nomination to fill the remainder of Martin's term of office. Glass sought and won five additional terms in the U.S. Senate without once facing a primary opponent (see Appendix IV).

Having completed the conversion of one political antagonist, the Organization then turned to the tasks of defeating another foe and recapturing the governorship. An obscure but loyal state legislator, E. Lee Trinkle, was selected to carry the Organization's banner in the 1921 gubernatorial primary. He was opposed by Harry St. George Tucker, who had unsuccessfully run for governor more than a decade earlier. Tucker was a man of wide experience and considerable popularity, and he

[20] Dabney, _Virginia,_ pp. 468–69.
[21] Ibid., pp. 470–71.
[22] For a full accounting of Glass's conversion, as well as a complete review of his long career in Virginia politics, see Harry Edward Poindexter, "From Copy Desk to Congress: The Pre-Congressional Career of Carter Glass" (Ph.D. diss., University of Virginia, 1966).

was a familiar personage to the state's voters. But he also was a machine opponent and was supported by Governor Davis. By selecting Trinkle, the Organization sought also to derail Davis's Senate ambitions. Despite all of Tucker's qualifications and advantages, Trinkle scored a surprisingly large victory in securing a 57.6 percent majority. Tucker fared much more poorly than he had in 1909. The machine had once again demonstrated its potency, and Westmoreland Davis was the biggest loser. His bid for the U.S. Senate nomination in 1922 against incumbent Claude Swanson was crushed by the massive margin of 73 percent to 27 percent.[23] The Organization, aided by the state's primary system, was again the complete master of the Virginia political scene.

Women's Suffrage Threatens the Primary

Aside from electoral politics, several other events had developed which affected the Old Dominion's primary. The Nineteenth Amendment to the U.S. Constitution which had granted women's suffrage in 1920 caused considerable consternation in Virginia. First it was widely feared that the amendment would give the vote to black women, and much discussion in the 1920 session of the General Assembly was devoted to this potential problem. Congressman Hal Flood found it necessary to remind his associates of section 19 of the 1902 state Constitution which provided for suffrage restrictions by means of age and residency requirements, property qualifications, and proof of literacy subject to the interpretation of local registrars. "It did it in 1902 and '03 in the case of negro male voters, and it will do it again." The General Assembly duly noted Flood's advice, and passed a resolution by overwhelming margins in both houses to add an amendment to the state Constitution applying section 19 and other 1902 voting restrictions to both men and women. It went into effect on the same day as the ratification of the Nineteenth Amendment to the federal Constitution—August 26, 1920.[24]

Still, women's suffrage—even suffrage for white women only—seemed to cause nightmares for some Organization stalwarts. They feared the alleged independence of women voters would undermine the machine's base of support. Unsuccessful efforts were made in some states to abandon primaries and return to conventions, since the latter were supposedly more easily controlled. There were persistent rumors in Virginia

[23] Kirby, pp. 155–58.
[24] Andrew Buni, *The Negro in Virginia Politics, 1902–1965* (Charlottesville: University Press of Virginia, 1967), pp. 75–77.

that the Organization in some quarters also desired a return to the convention system.[25] Apparently these rumors were not wholly without substantiation. Richard E. Byrd, author of the original primary law in Virginia and Organization kingpin, wrote an associate that he had changed his beliefs and had begun to favor the convention system:

The direct primary is an assault upon the representative idea. I believe that in the long run the representative system is the safest basis of a democracy. If the people are incapable of selecting honored and capable agents they will be even more incapable of exercising governmental powers by direct attention. . . .

While the convention system, like any human institution, is subject to abuse, it is, taking it altogether, the best known system of nominating party candidates. Under the primary it cannot be said that the people have any more control of their political affairs than they exercised under the convention plan. Certainly the primary has not put better men in office. If this is true, no reason for its continued existence can be justly urged.[26]

It quickly became obvious, however, that the price for such a change of heart might be too great for the Organization to pay. The Richmond *Times-Dispatch* issued a virtual call to arms when it heard the "incredible rumor" of the primary's impending demise: "If this rumor is based on fact—and there is strong reason to believe it is—the machine is so conscious of the growing revolt against it that it . . . is prepared to steam-roll the primary plan into obliteration and to set up a well-bossed, goose-stepping convention in its stead. . . . If it is more than a rumor, then the people of Virginia will have to take up arms to save their State from her ring-politicians."[27]

The threatened primary "obliteration" never materialized, but the "growing revolt" of citizens against the machine never took on any considerable proportions either. In the 1925 gubernatorial election, state Senator Harry Flood Byrd of Winchester, namesake nephew of the late congressman and state party chairman, swept to a landslide victory over state Senator G. Walter Mapp of Accomac of the Eastern Shore. Byrd, who had succeeded his uncle as party chairman, received 61.4 percent of the vote and was quickly acknowledged by most of the politically astute as the new machine boss. In the same primary, Junius E. West was unopposed for a second term as lieutenant governor, and the incumbent attorney general, John R. Saunders, won his third term with a 75.1

[25] Pidgeon, p. 24.
[26] Ibid., pp. 82–85, quoting Byrd to H. G. Peters, a prominent Democrat in Bristol, Va., Mar. 8, 1921.
[27] Sept. 19, 1924.

percent majority.[28] Women's suffrage, then, had very little effect on the
Organization's fortunes, and the early fears of machine associates were
unfounded. The continuation of the primary system was never seriously
threatened again during the life of the machine. Under the leadership of
the youthful and innovative Governor Byrd, the Organization had taken
out a new lease on its political life. There would be problems, for sure,
but Byrd and his followers would usually handle them ingeniously.

[28] West had first won election to the post in 1921 in a four-way contest—the largest
number of contestants in any statewide primary to that time, and a number never exceeded
and equaled only three times (in 1949 for governor and in 1969 for lieutenant governor and
attorney general). In 1921 West received 41.0 percent of the vote for lieutenant
governor. In the same election, incumbent attorney general John R. Saunders was
unopposed (see Appendix III).

Chapter 5

Separatism, Party Loyalty, and the White Primary

A MAJOR problem in the operation of the primary confronted the Organization during Byrd's tenure as governor. The "Catch 22" logic of its solution, as devised by the machine's leaders, has delighted observers of Virginia politics for decades, while causing more than a little consternation among advocates of party regularity and loyalty. The problem developed after the 1928 presidential election where, for the first time since the Reconstruction period, Virginia had voted for the Republican national ticket. The influence of Bishop Cannon, support of prohibition, and the fear of the alien influences surrounding the "wet" and Catholic Democratic presidential nominee, Alfred E. Smith of New York, combined to produce the GOP victory. Thousands of formerly loyal Democrats had voted for Herbert Hoover, but their one "indiscretion" presented difficulties for them in the 1929 Democratic gubernatorial primary. The party "loyalty oath," requiring a primary voter's pledge that he or she supported the party's nominees in the previous general election, has already been reviewed. A straight reading of the oath as it appeared in both statute and party plan seemed clearly to bar the "Democrats for Hoover" from voting in the 1929 primary.

An Interpretation of Law and Politics

The Organization saw the necessity of luring its strays back to the fold, lest the separation become a permanent one. A scenario was developed to remove the apparent legal obstacles. The state Democratic executive committee requested an official opinion on the subject from the Organization attorney general, John R. Saunders, in early 1929. Saunders replied in part:

I have carefully examined chapter 15 of the Code of Virginia, entitled, "Primary Elections." I do not deem it necessary for the purposes of this opinion to quote many of the sections contained in this chapter, but will only quote such portions of those sections which bear directly upon the question at issue.

The first sentence contained in section 222 reads as follows:

"This chapter shall apply to the nomination of candidates for such offices as shall be nominated by a direct primary and to no other nominations." The first sentence in section 226 is as follows:

"This chapter shall not apply to the nominations of presidential electors, nor to the nominations of candidates to fill vacancies, unless the candidates for nomination to fill vancancies are to be voted for on the date set by this chapter for regular primaries."

After a careful reading of those portions of sections 222 and 226 above quoted, and other provisions contained in the primary law, I am of the opinion that the right of a Democrat to participate in the August 1929 primary is not to be tested by the vote of such person for presidential electors in the 1928 presidential election, and Democrats who voted against the Democratic electors in the 1928 election, if otherwise qualified, are entitled to vote in the August 1929 primary election.[1]

Thus the problem was solved, at least to the satisfaction of the Organization if not the legal scholars. Saunders was forced to ignore several major statutory and party clauses to reach his conclusion. As James Latimer has noted, "It is still a matter of some wonder and controversy how Saunders could reach such a solemn conclusion, in view of the language of the party plan which then and now says the Virginia State Democratic convention 'shall *nominate* so many Presidential electors as the state of Virginia is entitled to. . . .' The explanation may lie in the sovereign state party theory that national party nominees are *not* necessarily state party nominees."[2]

There was, perhaps, one small precedent on which Saunders could have based his opinion. In May 1911 the State Democratic Central Committee refused requests by anti-Organization U.S. Senate candidates Carter Glass and William A. Jones to deny a primary vote to anyone who had not supported the 1908 Democratic presidential slate. Instead, the committee decided to continue its "existing policy of permitting any elector who promised to support the party nominee to vote in the primary." But the Byrd primary law passed the following year would certainly appear to have negated the "existing policy" by requiring retroactive party loyalty as well as future adherence.[3]

---

[1] Saunders to the Democratic Executive Committee, Jan. 31, 1929, in *Report of the Attorney General to the Governor of Virginia, 1928–29* (Richmond, 1929), pp. 96–97.

[2] James Latimer, "Virginia Politics, 1950–1960" (MS, 1961), pp. 30–31, quoted in Wilkinson, pp. 217–18.

[3] Moger, p. 224; *Acts of the Assembly, 1914*, c. 305, p. 516, section 8(b).

The Charade Continues

Equally fascinating were the subsequent opinions by four other attorneys general reaffirming Saunders's dubious legal ruling. In 1938 Abram P. Staples upheld Saunders by reasoning that "there have been five sessions of the General Assembly held since the above interpretation of the statute, but its provisions have not been amended." Further, he noted that the "official definition of the meaning of the words 'nominees of the party' was acquiesced in and adopted by the Democratic Party authorities in conducting the 1929 primaries, and must be deemed to be the sense and meaning which the party itself attributes to said words." When Robert Whitehead, anti-Organization leader and member of the House of Delegates, challenged the previous interpretations in 1952, J. Lindsay Almond, Jr., was able to discern a definitive distinction between presidential electors and all other party nominees: "It is clear that the language refers to those who have been nominated by a political party for congressional, state and local offices." Almond added, perhaps facetiously, "To my knowledge, no one has ever urged a contrary view." Even in the early 1960s the Organization attorney general continued to keep the faith. Albertis S. Harrison, Jr., reaffirmed the decision in 1960, and Robert Y. Button upheld all his predecessors by citing again the length of time which had passed without a successful challenge of the ruling in either party or legislature. Button was replying to a letter from the secretary of the Tazewell County electoral board in the party-conscious "Fightin' Ninth" District, who had been so bold as to ask, "[Does] this section of the law mean what it says or not?"[4]

It apparently did not. As a result of Saunders's novel opinion, majorities of the Richmond city Democratic committee have openly endorsed and supported the Republican presidential ticket in several elections.[5] Similar events have occurred in many other parts of Virginia. In general, then, a Democrat in the Old Dominion "can vote for a Communist or a Fascist or a Hottentot for President—if such extremes were available on the ballot— and still remain a Democrat in good standing so long as he went along with the Democratic nominees for State and Local Office."[6] The Virginia precedent established by Attorney General Saunders was not duplicated

[4] *Opinions of the Attorney General and Report to the Governor of Virginia, 1938–39* (Richmond: Division of Purchase and Printing, 1939), pp. 85–86; *Opinions of the Attorney General, 1952–53* (Richmond, 1953), p. 91; *Opinions of the Attorney General, 1960–61* (Richmond, 1961), pp. 122–23; *Opinions of the Attorney General, 1961–62* (Richmond, 1962), pp. 92–93.

[5] Richmond *Times-Dispatch*, May 2, 1970.

[6] Latimer, p. 31, quoted in Wilkinson, p. 218.

throughout the South. In fact, in many southern states, Democrats who had bolted the party in 1928 to support Hoover were ruled ineligible to run for Democratic nominations in the 1930 primaries.[7]

Effects of the Decision

The 1929 Saunders decision was an important one which affected the development of the state's Democratic party, the results of future primary elections, and the voting habits of many Virginians. The road was paved for Harry Bryd, Sr.'s policy of "golden silence" on Democratic presidential nominees—a policy which tacitly accepted and even encouraged the support of Republican national tickets. This separation of the state party from its national counterpart and the concurrent de-emphasis on loyalty to the national party was in large measure responsible for the stability and equilibrium which the Organization achieved and maintained over several decades. The separatist doctrine kept Virginia's conservatives in the Democratic party and out of the GOP, and thus continued dominance of the primary by the Organization was assured. By both blurring the distinction between the Democrats and the Republicans on the state level and emphasizing the distinction between national Democrats and Virginia Democrats, the Byrd Organization encouraged the development of ticket-splitting and independent voting habits which were to become even more predominant in later years. Virginia's lack of any system of party registration further accelerated this trend, as did the occasional calls for help by Organization leaders to Republican voters whenever the machine candidate found himself in some electoral difficulty.[8]

Virginia's unique election calendar also promotes and facilitates the separation of state from the federal party level.[9] The Commonwealth's governor is elected in the year after the presidential election. The House of Delegates is chosen the year after and the year before the presidential election, and the state Senate is also selected the year before every presidential race. The U.S. Constitution sets the election dates for the U.S.

[7] V. O. Key, Jr., *Politics, Parties, and Pressure Groups* (5th ed., New York: Thomas Y. Crowell Company, 1964), p. 392.

[8] Wilkinson, pp. 211–15. The most overt call for help ever issued to the GOP by the Byrd machine occurred in 1949, when Organization candidate John S. Battle was seriously threatened by Francis P. Miller in a four-way race. Republicans were also inclined to participate in the Democratic primary whenever Harry Byrd, Sr., was challenged for his U.S. Senate seat.

[9] See State Board of Elections, *Virginia Election Laws, As Amended to July 1, 1976* (Code of Virginia, Title 24.1) (Richmond: Department of Purchases and Supplies, 1976).

Senate and House of Representatives, so that separation of these offices from a presidential election is not always possible. It is likely that Virginia would have tried to do so if it could have, however. Before the adoption of the Seventeenth Amendment to the federal Constitution, which established popular election for U.S. senators, the primary for Senate nominators in Virginia was held either simultaneously with the gubernatorial primary in the year after the presidential election or with the state legislative primaries in the year before the presidential race. There were considerable political justifications for this arrangement from the perspective of the dominant Democrats. First, this election calendar enabled state officers to avoid both unwanted entanglements with the national party and the larger voter turnout which a presidential election always draws. Second, off-year elections denied to the Republican party the benefits which accrue from "coattail" voting. In 1928, for example, Virginia might well have elected some Republicans to statewide office while it was delivering its presidential electoral votes to Herbert Hoover had there been a simultaneous election for state and national posts. Only three other states—Kentucky, Mississippi, and New Jersey—have long provided for odd-year elections, and in 1975 Louisiana became the fourth.[10]

The strategy underlying the Saunders party loyalty opinion proved successful in 1929. John Garland Pollard, a former independent who had been absorbed by the Organization, was its candidate for governor. G. Walter Mapp was again the major opposition. If the bolt to Hoover had left anyone in doubt as to whether the machine still controlled the Virginia political stage, then the 1929 Democratic primary put those doubts to rest. With the help of thousands of "Hoovercrats," Pollard won a smashing victory, securing 75.4 percent of the vote, the largest proportion yet achieved by an Organization gubernatorial candidate. The popular James H. Price ran unopposed in the primary for lieutenant governor, and John R. Saunders was also without competition as he won his fourth term. In a general election larded with far more intrigue than usual, Pollard defeated Republican William Moseley Brown, a

---

[10] Council of State Governments, *The Book of the States, 1974–75* (Lexington, Ky.: Council of State Governments, 1974), pp. 32–34; and *Book of the States, 1972–73*, pp. 30–32. New Jersey elects its state officers on the same calendar as Virginia. Mississippi and Kentucky elect their governors and other state officers in the year before the presidential election. Until 1975 Louisiana also had nonsimultaneous state and national elections, although they occurred in the same year. State officers in Louisiana were elected in early February of presidential years, while the national elections did not take place until November. Since 1975 Louisiana has also elected its governor in the year before the presidential race. Wisconsin elects its state Supreme Court and a few other minor state officers in odd years.

prohibitionist backed by Bishop Cannon and the "anti-Smith Democrats," by more than 70,000 votes.[11] The Republican threat that had loomed large after Hoover's victory was thus defanged, and the supremacy of both Organization and primary was assured by the ingenious device of state and national party separatism.

The Loyalty Oath Endures

Despite the lessening of the loyalty oath's potence in presidential elections, the oath was regarded as a serious pledge of honor not be taken lightly with respect to state party nominees. The Democratic party, in its plan adopted in convention on June 9, 1932, had given its state, district, and local committees the power to direct the primary election judges to require every voter's written subscription to the following pledge of honor: "I, . . ., do state on my sacred honor that I am a member of the Democratic party and believe in its principles; that I voted for all of the nominees of said party at the next preceding general election in which I voted and in which the Democratic nominee or nominees had opposition; and that I shall support and vote for all the nominees of said party in the next ensuing general election." The judges could refuse to give a ballot to anyone not subscribing to the oath in toto. Attorney General Staples upheld the legality of the party's power to do this, and commented: "While, of course, in the absence of a resolution by the committee, it is not necessary for voters in the primary to subscribe and take the above pledge, nevertheless, it is generally understood that all persons offering to vote shall support and vote for all of the nominees of the party in the next ensuing general election." Several years later Attorney General Almond reaffirmed his predecessor's statement and described the loyalty obligations of the primary voter in even more serious tones: "The fact that the voter is not challenged does not alter the fact that through his participation he has represented himself to be qualified to vote in the Primary and that he will support all of the nominees. While the obligation thus assumed is not one which can be legally enforced, yet in ethics, good conscience and honor it far transcends legal considerations." That the Democratic party could effect such binding pledges is an indication of the authority vested in it by the Virginia primary law.[12]

[11] Dabney, *Virginia*, pp. 486–88.

[12] "Primary Plan of the Democratic Party" of 1932, as quoted in the *Opinions of the Attorney General, 1939–40* (Richmond, 1940), pp. 66–67; *Opinions of the Attorney General, 1951–52* (Richmond, 1952), pp. 68–69; Code of Virginia (1950), Code §24.1-172. Much of

A binding oath described by such weighty terms as "ethics," "conscience," and "honor" could not be easily dismissed by some Virginia Democrats in all national elections, notwithstanding the opinions of Organization attorneys general. The state versus federal party distinction was not always convincing to party members in the Commonwealth, as Harry Byrd was to discover in 1948. Byrd was strongly opposed to President Harry Truman's bid for the Democratic nomination that year, and he and Organization Governor William Tuck sought to pass a bill in the General Assembly which soon became known as the Anti-Truman Bill. The state Democratic party convention or a delegated special "party committee" (probably to be composed of the machine leadership) would have been given the power to determine for whom Virginia's Democratic electors would be instructed after the Democratic national convention. A provision was included which could have kept the official Democratic ticket off the ballot entirely. There was a virulent negative reaction from the anti-Organization forces and from Southwest Virginia, whose Democratic congressman, John W. Flannagan, loudly protested the impending coup. Normally, this hue and cry would not have been sufficient to deter the Organization. But the party loyalty oath, which supposedly did not apply to presidential elections, was responsible for a rare defeat of the machine. Public and press reaction not dissimilar to that which met the 1924 "rumors" of the primary's demise, as well as the disapproval of many "straight-ticket" Organization men, forced Byrd and Tuck to accept a very modified proposal. As passed, the bill guaranteed that the Democratic candidate's name would appear on the ballot, although the state party convention would be allowed to nominate a separate slate of Democratic electors pledged to another candidate whenever the nominees or platform of the national party proved "unacceptable."[13]

The loyalty oath also helped Truman to win a stunning November upset over Republican Thomas E. Dewey in Virginia. After Truman had been nominated by the Democrats, Byrd maintained a public silence of disapproval, while Tuck was outspokenly anti-Truman and supportive of the Dixiecrat forces of Strom Thurmond. The loyalty oath was also required of all candidates in the Democratic party primary, and contestants for U.S. Senate and House seats in 1948 were challenged heatedly on their November intentions. Finally, U.S. Senator A. Willis Robertson and most

---

the party's authority is derived from a clause in the primary law which states: "Each party shall have the power to make its own rules and regulations . . . and perform all functions inherent in such organizations."

[13] For a fuller discussion of the bill and developments surrounding it, see Wilkinson, pp. 79–80, and Key, *Southern Politics*, pp. 336–37, 436.

of the other Organization primary candidates endorsed Truman. To the consternation and embarrassment of Senator Byrd, his White House nemesis carried the Old Dominion by more than 28,000 votes.

The confusion and political intrigues engendered by the loyalty oath were not restricted to Virginia. The other southern states utilized such a pledge, and disenchantment with the drift of the national Democratic party caused difficulties in virtually all of Dixie. Loyalty oaths for primary candidates as well as voters were also universal in the South.[14] Virginia's candidate oath was revised in 1932 to add this mandatory declaration: "If I am defeated in the primary I hereby direct and irrevocably authorize the election officials charged with the duty of preparing the ballots to be used in the succeeding general election not to print my name on said ballots." This requirement kept defeated primary candidates from running in the general election as Independents. As such, it was yet another legal ruse to maintain the electoral primacy of the primary. Key stressed that "it is fundamental to Democratic supremacy in the South that the party's nominees shall go without effective challenge in the general election," and loyalty oaths for Democratic candidates and voters helped to ensure that eventuality. The candidate oath is particularly important since "its grand effect is to re-enforce the rule that the sole channel to political advancement is the Democratic party."[15]

Virginia's primary participation requirements are also similar to standards existing throughout the South. In general, anyone eligible to vote in the general election is eligible to participate in the primary.[16] Party membership and affiliation are required, of course, but this prerequisite is often ignored. Often the problem is a failure to define party membership in any meaningful way. In Virginia (and in Tennessee as well) it has proved particularly meaningless since Republicans have on occasion been invited to participate in the primary by the Democratic Organization and urged to do so by GOP leaders. This behavior highlights a major difference between the closed primary of the North and the closed primary of the South. In northern states where the GOP was traditionally strong, Democrats feared raids on their primary, whereby an influx of a large number of Republicans could affect the election result. Accordingly, Democrats often made serious attempts to keep the primary vote "pure." In the South,

[14] Key, *Southern Politics*, pp. 428–29, 433–34.

[15] *Acts of the Assembly, 1932*, c. 392, pp. 795–96. This provision was still in effect as of July 1, 1976; see *Virginia Election Laws, As Amended to July 1, 1976*, p. 96. Key, *Southern Politics*, pp. 424–25.

[16] Key, *Southern Politics*, p. 426. South Carolina is a partial exception to this generalization, as noted by Key.

by contrast, the GOP was too weak numerically to cause any real concern, and was even viewed as a potential resource by the dominant Democrats.

The White Primary

Virginia did differ considerably from its neighbors to the south in the development and demise of one particular institution—the white primary. Below the Mason-Dixon line existed a rigid, socially and legally enforced political segregation which matched the racial separatism in other phases of southern life. Adherence to racist doctrine was a hard and fast necessity for any politician, and the Southern progressive was no exception. C. Vann Woodward has capsuled the contradiction of Dixie progressivism in this way: "The joker in the Southern primaries was the fact that they were *white* primaries. Southern progressivism generally was progressivism for white men only. . . . The paradoxical combination of white supremacy and progressivism was not new to the region, but it never ceased to be a cause of puzzlement and confusion above the Potomac—and not a little, below." [17] The direct primary was not adopted per se to effect greater racial segregation in the nomination process. In the first place, most blacks were Republicans at that time in Virginia and the rest of the South. Further, the suffrage restrictions of the 1902 Constitution in the Old Dominion, and similar franchise impediments in other southern states, had already eliminated the bulk of Negroes from the polls. [18] Yet there may have been an indirect racial motive in the establishment of the primary since the primary has been construed to be "the fulfillment of the implied pledge of the disfranchisers that once the Negro was removed from political life the white men would be given more voice in the selection of their rulers." [19] It is doubtful that the Martin Organization would have

[17] C. Vann Woodward, *Origins of the New South, 1877-1913* (Baton Rouge: Louisiana State University Press, 1951), p. 373.

[18] Key comments that "although the possibility of excluding the Negro from the primary may have had something to do with its attractiveness, the significance of that factor in the adoption of the primary has never been investigated and weighed carefully. The primary, in effect, superseded a Democratic nominating process from which Negroes were already excluded partially by the fact that they were mostly Republicans. The movement of whites into the Democratic party and the taboo against general election challenge of the nominees had the effect of removing the threat of a Negro balance of power between whites in the general election. Yet even that threat had been taken care of fairly generally by other means before the statewide direct primary came into use" (*American State Politics*, pp. 90-91n).

[19] Woodward, p. 372.

assented to the progressive reformers at the 1904 Democratic state convention had the electorate not been "cleansed" and reduced two years earlier. So there is a reasonable though indirect connection between the adoption of the primary system in Virginia and the often-expressed desires of leading citizens to establish a pure, white electorate.

The history of the white primary in the Old Dominion is not dissimilar from that of its sister southern states in its early development.[20] An attempt was made at the May 1905 state Democratic convention held in Richmond to exclude blacks from the primaries through a proposed amendment to the state's election law restricting the primary franchise to whites. Yet many Democrats in Virginia, unlike their brethren in other southern states, saw the danger in this approach. A clear, statutory provision for voting discrimination would invite a legal test in the courts since the conflict with the Fifteenth Amendment to the U.S. Constitution was obvious. On the other hand, the Democratic party was construed at that time to be a private organization which could discriminate if it wished. As long as the exclusion of black voters came about because of party, and not statutory, regulation, there was a lessened chance of court intervention. The General Assembly was persuaded to ignore the Democratic party request. When a comprehensive primary law was finally enacted in 1912, no mention was made of racial matters in the statute. Instead, the party was granted wide discretion to regulate its affairs.[21] Already the state Democratic committee had ruled in May 1911 that only qualified white voters could participate in the approaching U.S. Senate primaries.[22] Yet a few of the "better sort" of Negroes had been allowed to vote.[23] But with the passage of the Byrd primary law, the primary polling booth was placed strictly off-limits to Virginia's black citizens. On February 13, 1913, the Democratic State Central Committee reaffirmed the white primary policy, and its decision was strengthened a short time thereafter in a legal opinion by Attorney General Pollard.[24] The 1911 ruling of the state central committee was officially adopted into the permanent Democratic Party Primary Plan on June 11, 1924, at the state convention in Norfolk.

[20] Much of the discussion on the white primary which follows is taken from Buni, pp. 60–120.

[21] There can be little doubt that the desire for a white primary was one of the chief motivations behind the far-reaching grant of power given to the party—a tradition which persisted long after the white primary was abolished and continues even today.

[22] Moger, p. 224n.

[23] Buni, p. 62.

[24] *Annual Report of the Attorney General to the Governor of Virginia, 1915* (Richmond, 1916), p. 27.

There were no sustained challenges by blacks to these maneuvers, a fact which may appear startling at first glance. But it must be remembered that blacks were far more concerned with the activities of the GOP, the party of Lincoln with which they had been associated since Reconstruction. Republicans in Virginia had also begun to adopt "lily-white" regulations, actions which did cause a stir among Negroes. It is doubtful that many blacks could have legitimately passed the Democratic loyalty test either, especially in gubernatorial primaries, which were always preceded by presidential elections. Those relatively few blacks who did cast ballots after the 1902 Constitutional Convention voted overwhelmingly for the Republican national ticket. Social pressures in the heavily Republican Negro community also made it difficult for blacks to express a preference for the Democratic party. Even if a black citizen was willing to brave the condemnation of his peers, his application to vote in the Democratic primary was likely to be rejected. Small wonder, then, that the Democratic party was permitted to have its "great white party" without a significant fuss from the Negro population.

Blacks, however, gradually began to shift away from a pattern of Republican support. Negroes drifted toward the Democratic party during the period from 1922 to 1928 for a variety of reasons. Republican President William Howard Taft had sided with the segregationists in his party in 1908, and this policy was continued during the early 1920s by the next Republican president, Warren G. Harding. The shift among blacks could clearly be detected after the 1928 presidential campaign of GOP standard-bearer Herbert Hoover. In attempting to gain the votes of conservative southern Democrats alienated by their party's Roman Catholic and "wet" nominee, Hoover surpassed the segregationist actions of his Republican predecessors by promising a vigorous lily-white party policy. He continued to take this view after assuming the presidential mantle, and this, combined with the effects of the Great Depression, completed the transplant of black allegiance from Republican to Democratic party.

This change was occurring throughout the rest of the South as well, but one additional factor facilitated the black political reorientation in Virginia: the elimination of the Old Dominion's white primary. As early as 1928 blacks in some areas of the state were challenging their exclusion from the primary. In 1930 several blacks, contending they were Democrats, requested to vote in the City of Richmond's Democratic primary, but the election judges refused them ballots. These individuals brought suits in federal district court, which held in their favor, citing violations of the Fourteenth and Fifteenth amendments to the U.S. Constitution. The decision was appealed to the U.S. Circuit Court of

Appeals, and there affirmed.[25] The federal courts construed the primary as an official governmental function rather than an activity of a private organization, thus subjecting the Democratic primary to constitutional tests. They were able to do this in Virginia thanks to one of the progressive innovations in the Byrd primary law—public financing of the primary election. Otherwise, the statute had been carefully designed to leave wide discretion to the party with little direct state connection to the primary. Had it not been for the assumption of election expenses by the public treasury, Virginia's white primary might have endured another decade or so. Attorney General Saunders hopefully reminded an inquirer that "until a case involving the same question has reached the Supreme Court of the United States, it cannot positively be said that colored persons are entitled to vote in Democratic primaries." Yet he counseled, perhaps reluctantly, that "judges of primary elections who refuse colored persons the privilege of voting, where they have all other qualifications to participate in a Democratic primary save that of color, are liable to suit for damages in the United States courts."[26] Compliance with the court decisions was generally the rule throughout Virginia, and by 1936 eligible and registered blacks had no difficulty participating in Democratic primary elections.[27] The key words here are "eligible and registered" blacks. As long as the poll tax and other suffrage restrictions continued, the Organization had very little reason to worry, and this realization undoubtedly encouraged compliance with the new legal interpretation. The number of blacks on the voting rolls remained a small fraction of the total registered population.

Virginia was the only southern state in 1930 wholly without a racial restriction on primary participation. Even in Virginia, though, the moribund white primary was kept on the books in the Democratic party plan, as Key reported:

The Democratic party rules . . . continued in form to limit participation in the primaries to whites. They so provided even in 1947. At a recent convention the removal of the dead proscription from the party rules was considered by the leaders, who concluded that it would be preferable not to raise the issue. It would have created an opportunity for intolerant elements to sound off, unnecessarily and undesirably opening the whole race issue, which is little discussed in

[25] *West* v. *Bliley*, 33 F.2d 177 (E.D. VA. 1929); *Bliley* v. *West*, 42 F.2d 101 (Cir. Ct. of Appeals, 4th Cir., 1930). For a further discussion of these cases, see the text and footnotes in *Michie's Jurisprudence of Virginia and West Virginia*, 3 (Charlottesville: Michie Company, 1949): 937.
[26] *Report of the Attorney General to the Governor of Virginia, 1930–31* (Richmond, 1931), p. 80.
[27] Buni, p. 106.

Virginia politics. Responsible party leaders counseled such action; meanwhile Negroes sat as members of the convention and participated in primaries.[28]

After first holding out some hope that the white primary was legal, the Supreme Court in 1944 struck down white primary statutes in *Smith v. Allwright,* holding that when the primary election of one party is, in effect, the final election, it becomes state action within the meaning of the Fifteenth Amendment.[29] Any rules or regulations made by the decision-making bodies of the party in such a situation are as subject to constitutional limitations as actions of the state legislature. Compliance was not the rule in most southern states, in contrast to Virginia, and many state legislatures used delaying tactics and legal strategems in continuing to oppose even a modicum of Negro participation in their primaries.[30]

The Reformers Fail

The black voter participation rate in Virginia's primary was, proportionate to the Negro population, even more dismal than the turnout of the potential white vote. Yet no race or region in the Commonwealth could point to anything but a shockingly small number of persons participating in elections. This situation did prick the consciences of some citizens, and several state newspapers editorialized frequently on the causes and cures. Nothing much came of their concern, despite legislative studies and gubernatorial proposals. Former independent Governor Westmoreland Davis had vigorously attacked the poll tax in 1937 in an agricultural magazine of which he was publisher, with little effect. Governor James H. Price, another independent-minded chief executive, had expressed his discouragement about the low voter turnouts in his 1938 inaugural address, in a 1940 address to the General Assembly, and in many public appearances throughout the state. It was his conviction that "a substantially restricted suffrage was incompatible with the existence of a real political democracy." Accordingly, he proposed to the legislature some modest reforms in the poll tax, seeking to reduce both the amount of the tax from $1.50 to $1.00 and fraudulent payments of the tax as well. When the legislature refused to grant either proposal, Price asked for a study from the Virginia Advisory Legislative Council (VALC), and they were agree-

[28] Key, *Southern Politics*, pp. 620, 624. A few counties in North Carolina and Florida and most counties in Tennessee also did not have the white primary in 1930.
[29] *Grovey* v. *Townsend*, 295 U.S. 45 (1935); *Smith* v. *Allwright*, 321 U.S. 649 (1944).
[30] See Key's general history of the white primary in *Politics, Parties, and Pressure Groups*, pp. 601-12.

able. A VALC subcommittee was formed, headed by Professor Robert Kent Gooch of the University of Virginia and including a Republican state senator, Ted Dalton of Radford, who would later play a major role in preparing the groundwork for a competitive two-party system in Virginia. After a thorough review of electoral laws and practices, the subcommittee recommended the elimination of the poll tax as a prerequisite for voting and a redesign of the registration system so that "a fair, just, and impartial test of genuine literacy" could be established. The Organization-controlled VALC kept the report under wraps and killed it by a vote to take "no action."[31]

This result is hardly surprising, of course. Suffrage restrictions were crucial to the continued success of the Organization. The poll tax and other strictures made a primary worthwhile and an electorate manageable for the Organization. The machine could hardly be expected to yield or even modify them voluntarily. The suffrage structure in Virginia made the political system a stable and durable one. The system could absorb a number of "shocks" like the white primary and loyalty oath controversies discussed above without losing its equilibrium. It was this suffrage structure which sustained the Organization and its primary for six decades.

[31] See Robert Kent Gooch, esp. pp. 6, 15–16.

Chapter 6

The Organization's Convention Affair

IN REVIEWING the primary election results of the period from 1933 to 1946, it is difficult to tell that major political controversies on party loyalty, the white primary, and state party separatism were raging. The Organization's candidates consistently won clear and convincing victories, the only exception being James H. Price's successful quest for the governorship in 1937 as an anti-Organization candidate (and even in that case he was soon cut to pieces by the machine). Politics in the Old Dominion seemed so predictable that one wonders how the voters managed to stay awake. Behind the scenes, of course, political maneuverings were as frantic as ever, and the machine found it necessary from time to time to make accommodations and adjustments. But a smooth and successful result for the Organization always seemed inevitable. The Byrd forces even found an opportunity to flirt with the convention nominating process, an event precipitated by legal technicalities and not a few political considerations.

A String of Machine Victories

In 1933 Claude Swanson vacated his U.S. Senate seat from Virginia to accept the post of secretary of the navy in newly elected President Franklin D. Roosevelt's cabinet. To no one's surprise, former governor and Organization leader Harry F. Byrd, Sr., was appointed to the vacancy. Byrd ran unopposed for the Democratic nomination for the one year remaining in Swanson's term in 1933 and bowled over his Republican opponent in November, gathering 71.3 percent of the vote. He again ran unopposed for renomination in 1934 and was elected to his first full term in the Senate with 76.0 percent of the vote against Republican opposition. Yet another unopposed renomination in the primary greeted Byrd in 1940. The placidity of the 1933 Democratic Senate primary was barely disturbed by the simultaneous gubernatorial contest. Organization favorite George C. Peery of Tazewell, who had "redeemed" the Ninth District congressional seat from the GOP in 1922 and who had later served as a member of the State Corporation Commission, crushed two opponents with 61.6 percent of the vote. The governor's race was the only primary contest, since both Lieutenant Governor James H. Price and Attorney General John R. Saunders were unopposed for renomination.

The Organization found it necessary to accommodate popular Lieutenant Governor Price in the next gubernatorial primary. He was not a Byrd favorite, the result of his independent mind, but his following across the state was such that he was unbeatable.[1] Price was not totally unacceptable, so the Organization fell into line behind him. In the primary contest, Price received the largest vote percentage of any opposed candidate in the history of the Virginia primary, an incredible 86.1 percent in defeating Norfolk's Vivian L. Page. This mark was never to be exceeded. An Organization state senator, Saxon W. Holt, became lieutenant governor with 56.7 percent of the vote, and Abram P. Staples won the first of three terms as attorney general with 54.8 percent.[2]

The Organization steamroller continued in the wartime elections of 1941 and 1945. Colgate W. Darden, Jr., of Norfolk, a former congressman and future president of the University of Virginia, was chosen by the machine for governor in 1941. He won in a walk with 76.6 percent of the vote over two opponents. William M. Tuck gave the Organization even more reason to rejoice with his defeat of anti-Organization leader Moss A. Plunkett for lieutenant governor. Tuck received 81.3 percent of the vote, a margin in the annals of Virginia primary history second only to Price's 1937 victory. It was little surprising when Tuck was chosen to succeed Darden in 1945.[3] Moss Plunkett was again Tuck's opponent, but the antimachine independent bettered his 1941 showing only slightly. Tuck was elected with 70.1 percent of the vote. The race for lieutenant governor in 1945 became a donnybrook for the Organization, despite the fact that a loyal machine man won. The Byrd forces had made the mistake of allowing two Organization legislators, Charles R. Fenwick and L. Preston Collins, to battle it out in the primary. It was a hotly contested election, and when the votes were counted, Fenwick was declared the winner by 572 votes, a narrow plurality win of 38.3 percent to Collins's 37.8 percent (Leonard G. Muse, an independent, received 23.9 percent of the vote). However, in examining the election returns, Collins spotted some peculiar totals from Wise County, in his home area: Fenwick, 3,307; Muse, 164; Collins, 122. Ballot fraud in an area notorious for such

[1] Price was known as a "conservative New Dealer" while Byrd was opposed to most major programs of President Roosevelt's administration.

[2] The candidates in the lieutenant governor and attorney general primaries tried their best to attach themselves to Price's coattails. They often argued about who had endorsed Price the earliest and the most feverently.

[3] Tuck was to become one of the most colorful Virginia governors in modern times. See Wilkinson, pp. 24–42, and Dabney, *Virginia*, pp. 516–20.

electoral swindles was apparent. Collins contested the election in the courts, and Judge Julian Gunn of Richmond sought to inspect the county's poll books. When Wise officials reported that twenty-four of the twenty-six books had been mysteriously "stolen," Gunn threw out the county's entire vote, thus making Collins the winner of the primary nomination. The publicity from all this was none too favorable to the Organization, especially since the machine prided itself and the state on electoral integrity. A valuable lesson had been learned by the Organization leadership.

The Convention Fling of 1946

Perhaps with this recent unpleasant experience in mind, the Organization found reason to break with the four-decade-old primary tradition in 1946.[4] U.S. Senator Carter Glass died during his fifth term on May 28, aged 88. His health had been in decline for some time, and so his death was not unexpected. The leadership of the Democratic party almost immediately declared that the nominee to fill the remainder of the Glass term must be chosen by convention. They contended that the law made no provision for a special primary or for candidates to enter the previously scheduled regular August primary after the filing date (which was May 7 of that year). The regular primary of 1946 already had a Senate contest. Harry Byrd was being challenged for the first time since he had been appointed to the Senate seat in 1933 by a vigorous anti-Organization candidate, Martin Hutchinson.

The leadership's interpretation of the Virginia statutes was not unchallenged. There was a considerable dispute about whether a primary could be called, since the law was ambiguous at best on the subject. Norman R. Hamilton, editor of the Portsmouth *Star* and former Second District congressman, called for a primary, as did anti-Organization leader Moss Plunkett and Byrd's opponent, Martin Hutchinson. The Richmond *Times-Dispatch* in an editorial entitled "Let the People Speak!" vehemently demanded a primary: "It is impossible to find any non-legal reason why the Democratic candidate for . . . Senate . . . should be chosen in a convention, rather than a primary. Conventions are notoriously subject to manipulation by machines. . . . If the party leaders insist upon proceeding with their plans for a convention, it will mean that

---

[4] The details of the 1946 convention which follow are derived from newspaper accounts appearing in the Richmond *Times-Dispatch* and the Norfolk *Virginian-Pilot*, May 28–Sept. 8, 1946.

the nomination will be cooked up in some smoke-filled room, with the outcome decided in advance and merely ratified on the convention floor."[5] The machine counterattacked, with state party chairman Horace H. Edwards of Richmond as spokesman. He insisted that the Organization was still loyal to the primary nomination method, but the legal technicalities clearly prevented a primary in this case. But, as the *Times-Dispatch* observed, "The machine . . . can find a way to choose Virginia's new Senator in a primary—if it wants to do so. But does it want to? It certainly doesn't, but it might be compelled to yield to the force of public opinion. Such miracles have happened before."[6]

There was to be no miracle in 1946, however. Gradually, Organization stalwarts publicly lined up behind the contention of the party chairman. Potential Senate candidates A. Willis Robertson and Howard W. Smith, both members of the U.S. House of Representatives, supported the calling of a convention. Smith remarked that "I believe in playing the game by the rules, and the rule for a convention apparently is beyond dispute." If it was not "beyond dispute" then, an official opinion by the Organization attorney general, Abram P. Staples, shortly thereafter did silence the discussion. Staples completely affirmed the pronouncements of party chairman Edwards.[7]

There were certain legal technicalities which legitimately served as justifications for abandoning the primary. Yet, as the *Times-Dispatch* had suggested, the Organization could have found a way to circumvent these technicalities even if it required a short special session of the General Assembly. As it was in 1946, there were very cogent reasons for not holding a primary to fill the Senate vacancy. The most important motive for favoring a convention was to ensure the renomination of the machine's boss, Harry Byrd. The Organization did not wish to complicate the Byrd-Hutchinson race in any way. In addition to this, the Organization's favored candidate for the Senate vacancy, Howard W. Smith, was up for renomination to his House seat, and would have been forced to

[5] May 31, 1946. The previous discussion in this study might lead one to argue that suffrage restrictions also left the primary "with the outcome decided in advance and merely ratified" on primary election day!

[6] June 1, 1946.

[7] Richmond *Times-Dispatch*, June 1, 1946; *Opinions of the Attorney General, 1945–46* (Richmond, 1946), pp. 61–62. Staples pointed to a part of the state party plan adopted in a 1944 Roanoke convention which took away the powers of nomination to fill vacancies from the State Democratic Central Committee and vested them instead in a convention. Staples concluded that there was no provision in the statutes permitting a special primary, and that even if there had been one, the Democratic party plan would not permit its exercise since a convention was required for vacancies.

abandon his reelection bid to run in a Senate primary. Smith was opposed at the time by three other candidates, none of them Organization-tilting, and of course the filing deadline had long since passed. If a Senate primary were held, the Organization would lose control of Smith's House seat, an unpalatable result to the machine. On the other hand, if Smith were nominated by a convention held after his primary renomination to the House seat, a district convention of Organization regulars would choose Smith's replacement.[8] Suspicions of these motivations are con-firmed in a party decision to hold a postprimary convention. This action deferred the political controversies and rivalries involved in choosing a new senator until after Byrd was safely renominated. It also allowed Smith to win renomination to his House seat.

The Organization Is Outmaneuvered

So a month after Byrd had crushed Hutchinson's bid for the Senate, a Democratic state convention gathered in Richmond on September 5, 1946.[9] There were 1,128 delegate votes, with a simple majority needed to nominate. Former governor Colgate W. Darden, Jr., was immensely popu-lar at the time and the real favorite of most of the convention delegates. He could not be persuaded to run, but his presence at the convention would unwittingly help to foil the Organization. Howard W. Smith, as earlier reported, was the choice of Organization kingpin Harry Byrd,[10] who found Smith even more conservative and anti-New Deal than himself. Representative A. Willis Robertson, a more moderate Organization man who had declared twice during the summer that he definitely would not be a candidate, finally decided to make the race and oppose Smith. As is the experience of many conventions, a half-dozen other candidates—favorite sons primarily—were formally nominated.[11]

[8] Another potential Senate contender, Rep. A. Willis Robertson, presented no similar problem to the Organization. Robertson was running unopposed for renomination to his House seat, so his seat would not have been lost to the Organization had he withdrawn to run in a Senate primary. A district convention to choose his successor would have been automatically necessitated.

[9] The account of the convention is taken from reports carried in the Richmond *Times-Dispatch* and the Norfolk *Virginian-Pilot*, Sept. 5–7, 1946. In the August senatorial primary, Byrd received 63.5 percent of the vote in defeating Hutchinson.

[10] A sure sign of Byrd's preference for Howard Smith was Smith's nomination at the con-vention by John S. Battle, an Organization leader who was to be the next machine governor.

[11] These included C. S. Carter of Bristol (favorite son of the Ninth District), state Senator Morton G. Goode (favorite son of the Fourth District), William A. Wright

The first ballot indicated the convention's strong Darden sentiments. The former governor received 316 votes to 203 for Smith, 148 for Robertson, and 459 for others.[12] At the end of the balloting, Darden withdrew his name from any further consideration by the convention. He had never consented to his name being placed in nomination and actually had to demand his right to withdraw. On the second ballot, there was a considerable shift of Darden support to Robertson, as Robertson won 358 votes to 318 for Smith and 450 for others.[13] On the third ballot, large numbers of delegates began switching to Robertson. Anti-Organization leader Moss Plunkett of Roanoke urged his delegates to join the Robertson camp to prevent Smith's nomination. Before the ballot was even completed, Howard Smith moved to nominate Robertson by acclamation.[14] In conceding defeat to the convention, Smith commented: "This evening we have seen a great demonstration of democracy at work. Free and untrammelled delegates have voted their free and untrammelled wishes." The delegates had proved too "free" from the Organization's standpoint, and the machine uncomfortably found itself outmaneuvered. Some would contend that the anti-Organization forces produced this setback for their foes. As Key reported:

A long story lay behind the sidetracking of Howard Smith. In August, 1946, at Covington in Alleghany County in far western Virginia, several CIO unions brought their members to the mass meeting to elect delegates to the state Democratic convention. They caught the local machine unprepared, controlled the meeting, and elected the delegates. . . .

Came the convention. The Alleghany delegates, occupying a strategic place on the alphabetical roll, yielded to the Nansemond County delegation which put in nomination former Governor Colgate W. Darden. The Governor was no crusader, no antiorganization man, but he enjoyed an enormous personal popularity and great respect throughout the state. His nomination threw the convention into an uproar, caused confusion, and gave opportunity to demonstrate the unacceptability of Representative Smith. Although Governor Darden did not desire the nomination, the maneuvers of the labor delegation from Alleghany and the restiveness of other delegations induced the high command to acquiesce in the

---

(the state's conservation commissioner and favorite son of the First District), and Harvey B. Apperson (a member of the State Corporation Commission).

[12] Breakdown of the "other" vote is: C. S. Carter, 166; Morton Goode, 134; William Wright, 110; and Harvey Apperson, 49.

[13] Breakdown of the "other" vote is: Carter, 181; Goode, 103; Wright, 102; and Apperson, 64.

[14] Robertson went on to become the state's junior U.S. senator in November by defeating Republican Robert H. Woods and several Independents easily. Robertson won his first six-year Senate term in 1948 after a primary challenge by James P. Hart, Jr. Robertson won 70.3 percent of the vote in that primary contest.

nomination of its second choice. Or, at least, such is the story of those who believe that they blocked the high command.[15]

Thus the Organization's first experience with the statewide nominating convention since 1901 proved less than successful. The irony, of course, was the Organization would probably have had a better chance of securing the nomination for its favorite in a primary than by the convention method which it chose. The anti-Organization forces, who had demanded a primary, exercised more influence in the workings and product of the 1946 convention than they had been able to do in a single primary for decades. This experience, and lesson, would not be lost on the Organization. The affair with the convention was over; the primary was held in warm embrace for the rest of the Organization's life.

[15] Key, *Southern Politics*, pp. 24–25.

Chapter 7

The Golden Age Continues

THE Organization came closer to losing the governor's chair in 1949 than it had at any time since the victory of Westmoreland Davis in the three-way contest of 1917. Yet, supported by the restricted suffrage base and saved by the influx of state Republicans, the machine retained control of the state executive office in 1949. A few adjustments were made in the primary law as a result, including the adoption of a runoff primary for which Virginia had never before seen a need. Then, reinvigorated to some extent by the policies of "Massive Resistance" to the racial decrees of the U.S. Supreme Court, the Organization rolled merrily along with the primary as its mode of transportation, as the golden age continued.

The 1949 Gubernatorial Primary

A split in the Organization's ranks and a highly regarded independent challenger combined to give the machine its greatest scare in three decades. John S. Battle of Charlottesville was the candidate of the Byrd forces, but there were also two other conservative candidates in the race—Horace H. Edwards of Richmond, former state party chairman and a maverick member of the Organization, and Remmie Arnold of Petersburg, a very conservative fountain pen manufacturer. The anti-Organization, by contrast, presented a united front in fielding Francis Pickens Miller, a respected former member of the House of Delegates.[1] Miller made a vigorous effort and, thanks to the split in the Organization, was thought to be leading Battle. This situation called for drastic action by the machine. First, Harry Byrd broke his personal precedent against public stands in such campaigns and leaped into the fray. Referring to the labor organizations supporting Miller, Byrd called Miller the "CIO-sponsored candidate" and at the same time cautioned machine adherents

[1] Never before had there been so many candidates in the party's gubernatorial primary, four, a number which would never again be equaled or surpassed. Only one other time had there been so many candidates in any primary, in the 1921 lieutenant governor's contest, and this number would be equaled only twice more (in the 1969 races for lieutenant governor and attorney general). See Dabney, *Virginia*, pp. 520–22, for an account of the campaign.

that "a vote for Edwards is a vote for Miller." Then Major Henry A. Wise, a former member of the GOP national committee, urged Republicans to enter the Democratic primary to vote for Battle. The Democrats not so subtly let it be known that the Republicans would be welcome. These two developments—the Byrd intervention and the Republican crossover—reversed the earlier trend to Miller. When the ballots were counted, Battle had edged Miller 42.8 percent to 35.3 percent. Edwards received about 15 percent and Arnold only 7 percent of the vote.

A Runoff Primary for Virginia

Much has been made of this near defeat of the Organization, and many histories cite this election as indicating severe deterioration of the machine. The 1949 gubernatorial primary signified nothing of the kind. Miller's percentage of the vote was not much different from those of several other antimachine candidates in the past.[2] In the same 1949 primary, Organization Lieutenant Governor L. Preston Collins of Marion defeated Nick Prillaman of Martinsville, an ally of Miller's, by 68.1 percent to 31.9 percent of the vote. The machine candidate for attorney general, J. Lindsay Almond, Jr., defeated perennial anti-Organization candidate Moss A. Plunkett of Roanoke by a similar margin, 66.8 percent to 33.2 percent. The problem was not machine deterioration but primarily one of a split in the Organization vote. It is likely that Battle would have received most of Edwards's and Arnold's votes had they not been in the race, thus resulting in a sizable victory for Battle. It certainly appears that most voters who cast a ballot for Edwards and Arnold also voted for Collins and Almond.[3] The problem for the Organization in 1949 was rather one of a multicandidate field, which had so rarely occurred in Virginia primaries. The difficulty was quickly remedied by the 1952 General Assembly, which enacted a runoff primary statute.[4] In the event one candidate in the first primary failed to receive a majority of the votes, a second, or runoff, primary would be held if requested by the runner-up. To accommodate the runoff, the first primary was moved from August to the second Monday in July. The second primary, if any,

[2] See Appendixes III and IV.
[3] This is surmised from the election percentages received by the candidates in each city and county. In almost all cases, the vote for Almond and Collins approximates the vote given Battle, Arnold, and Edwards together. The contention in the text could only be proved, of course, by a sample survey of 1949 primary voters—a poll which unfortunately does not exist.
[4] *Acts of the Assembly, 1952* (Richmond, 1952), c. 4, pp. 10–15.

would be held on the fifth Tuesday after the first primary, or some time in mid-August. The same statutes regulating the first primary were made applicable to the runoff, with the exception that no additional filing fees, signatures of voters, or declarations would be required of the candidates.

Virginia's runoff was unique in the South, not because it had been established, but rather because it had taken so long for the state to adopt it. The Old Dominion was the very last southern state to enact a statewide runoff statute. In most of Dixie, the runoff had been in effect almost as long as the primary.[5] Runoffs had been established as early as 1902 in Mississippi and as late as 1939 in Arkansas. Most of the South had incorporated the second primary in the period from 1915 to 1922. As statistics presented later in this study will show, Virginia was tardy in introducing a runoff because of a persistent bifactionalism which made the runoff unnecessary. The primary for each office was almost invariably limited to two major candidates, each of whom represented a fairly distinguishable faction.[6] The "winnowing out" process which occurred in each faction before the primary thus usually resulted in a two-way race, in which one candidate inevitably received a majority. Even when a third candidate filed for nomination, one factional candidate would normally receive a majority. Most campaign resources and constituency groups were monopolized by the two factions, leaving little room for maneuvering and few votes to the third candidate. The runoff primary, then, really was not necessary in Virginia, unlike in most of the other multifactional southern states where primaries sometimes had as many as a dozen candidates. Significantly, in the more than quarter century since its adoption in Virginia, the runoff has been utilized only twice—for the 1969 contests for governor and attorney general.

The provisions of the 1952 Virginia runoff statute were similar in some respects to those of other southern states. The typical interval between the first and second primaries was two to five weeks, and Virginia was at the latter end of that scale. In all of the South including Virginia, the second primary was not held if the runner-up in the first primary declined it. But in every other southern state except North Carolina, the runoff was automatically held barring a waiver from the primary runner-up. In Virginia, the runoff was not held unless the second-place finisher filed

[5] Council of State Governments, *The Book of the States, 1935* [*-1953*]. In Tennessee the runoff is used only in the unlikely event of a tie. As such, it can really be classified with Virginia, for much the same reason, bifactionalism.

[6] In this respect the primary developed a kind of two-party system within its structure, although the analogy is inaccurate in several major respects; see chap. 9 below.

an official request for it. Further, in all of Dixie except Georgia, Louisiana, and Mississippi, the runoff provision applied to all state and local offices. In the Old Dominion runoffs were mandatory only for the statewide elective offices of U.S. senator, governor, lieutenant governor, and attorney general. However, the General Assembly did give authority to district and local party committees even before 1952 to require nominations by majority vote.

Republicans Test the Primary Waters

While it was quite common for a nonsouthern Republican party to hold a primary election, it was exceedingly rare to find the southern GOP using the system. The Virginia state party was eligible to employ the primary nomination method at state expense, since it had repeatedly met the statutory requirement of 25 percent support in presidential elections.[7] Yet not a single statewide, congressional, or legislative district GOP primary had been held before 1947. Republicans preferred their traditional convention for a number of reasons. First of all, there was not an overwhelming degree of intraparty competition on any level, with the exception of a few areas where the party showed strength. Candidates for statewide office often had to be recruited by the party hierarchy. Not many individuals were eager to serve as sacrificial lambs, inevitably gored by the dominant Democrats. Second, the convention had real value to a party whose members were often discouraged and disheartened. The meetings sometimes seemed to take the form of revivals akin to those of fundamentalist religions as the group of true believers were exhorted to "keep the faith."[8] Further, party leaders feared the embarrassment of a low turnout if a primary were held. Casting a Republican ballot was socially and politically undesirable at best in most areas of Virginia—even a stigma in some places which could affect one's business, family, friends, and relationships. Fortunately for the GOP, the secret ballot in the general election protected Democratic defectors. The Republican vote in the general election was small relative to the Democratic turnout, but it would likely have been much smaller if voters were required to

---

[7] Only once since the establishment of the primary did the Republicans fall below the 30 percent level of support in a presidential election. In 1936 Republican Alf Landon received only 29.4 percent of the presidential vote. The Democrats came closest to the cutoff level for primary funding in 1972, when presidential nominee George McGovern received only 30.1 percent of the vote in Virginia.

[8] See columnist Charles McDowell's column, Richmond *Times-Dispatch,* May 2, 1970, p. B-1.

identify themselves by party affiliation before voting. In a primary election, however, a voter was identified by the party ballot he selected. Even some confirmed Republicans might hesitate to go to the polls under these conditions.

Nevertheless some Republicans, especially from the Northern Virginia region, began agitating within the party for a test of the primary nominating system. Their quest was made easier in 1946 when the Republican party altered its rules to add an optional primary clause which could be exercised on state, district, or local levels. An intraparty fight developed in 1948 in the Eighth Congressional District on whether to hold a primary later that year. In a pattern which was to be repeated in later primary discussions by the GOP, urban Republicans from Alexandria, Arlington, and Fairfax strongly advocated the primary, while Republicans from the rural parts of the district fought the change. One Albemarle County Republican warned his urban brethren: "Southern district Republicans would not turn out to vote in the traditionally Democratic area. A man would rather stick his hand in a furnace than ask for a Republican ballot."[9] The urban Republicans in the Eighth won the battle, however, and on August 3, 1948, the first major Republican primary election was held in Virginia. Two candidates filed for the congressional seat, and a total of 3,607 votes were cast in the GOP contest.[10] At the same time, though, the two-candidate Democratic contest in the Eighth District drew a vote of 15,530.[11] Of the total district voter turnout in the congressional races, then, Republicans had drawn only 18.8 percent; as few as 22 Republican votes were recorded in one county.[12]

Still, the performance must have been satisfactory enough to encourage the party to hold its first—and only as of 1975—statewide primary.[13] Walter Johnson of Heathsville was unopposed for the gubernatorial nomination, and received 8,888 votes. No candidate filed for the party's attorney general nomination.[14] The lone Republican contest was for the lieutenant

[9] Key, *Southern Politics*, p. 441.

[10] Tyrrell Krum received 2,478 votes (68.7 percent of the total) to defeat Charles O. Pratt, who won but 1,129 votes. See State Board of Elections, *Statement of the Vote for Members of Congress and United States Senator: Primary Election, August 3, 1948.* (Richmond: Division of Purchase and Printing, 1948).

[11] The incumbent congressman, Howard W. Smith, was challenged by Arthur F. Souther; Smith received 11,131 votes (71.7 percent) to Souther's 4,399 votes (ibid.).

[12] King George County produced this low Republican total. By contrast, 120 votes were cast for Democratic candidates.

[13] The primary was held on Aug. 2 simultaneously with the Democratic primary, as provided by law.

[14] The eventual Democratic nominee for attorney general, J. Lindsay Almond, Jr., actually tied for the highest number of Republican write-in votes (7) for the post.

governor's post. E. Thomas McGuire, an insurance man from Petersburg, defeated Berkeley Williams, a former Richmond postmaster, to secure the nomination. McGuire was favored by 4,635 voters (54.1 percent) to 3,930 for Williams. Some Republican leaders had helped to sabotage their maiden primary, of course, by urging party members to bail out Byrd candidate John Battle in the Democratic contest. Even considering this fact, the 1949 Republican primary can only be labeled an unqualified disaster. Only 2.7 percent of all 1949 primary voters had chosen to cast a Republican ballot. Twenty-two cities and counties had recorded less than 10 Republican votes, and one county (Charles City) reported not a single vote cast.[15] Even legislative primary contests held in Norfolk, Bedford County, and Fairfax County did not appear to increase the turnout substantially in those localities.[16] The unopposed and minimally opposed nature of the Republican primary, combined with an exciting and perceptively close Democratic contest, undoubtedly depressed the Republican totals. Despite these not unreasonable excuses, the Republican party was naturally embarrassed by the pitiful vote it had received. Its weak voter base was exposed for all to see. After this discouraging experience with the primary system, only one other major primary—in the Eighth Congressional District in 1950–has been conducted by the Republicans until recently.[17] Republican adherence to the convention system since their 1949 fiasco has continued to be virtually universal in Virginia, even to the present day.[18]

[15] These 22 counties, for the most part, were found in or near Southside Virginia, the stronghold of the Organization. Total Democratic vote was 316,622, compared to 8,888 votes for the Republicans. See State Board of Elections, *Statements of the Vote, Republican and Democratic Primary Elections, August 2, 1949* (Richmond: Division of Purchase and Printing, 1949).

[16] These were the first legislative primaries ever held by Republicans. Only a few have been held since then, all in Northern Virginia; see tables 1 and 3 in chap. 10.

[17] Republican turnout was again dismal, only 16.8 percent of the total votes cast in both primaries. This was a slight decrease from two years earlier, and the primary was discontinued in the district of its Republican birth after 1950. See State Board of Elections, *Statement of the Vote for Members of Congress: Primary Election, August 1, 1950* (Richmond: Division of Purchase and Printing, 1950).

[18] The Eighth District revived the GOP congressional primary once, in 1972. In that year a more respectable showing was made by the Republicans, indicating the growth of the party in that district. The 1972 GOP primary provided 11,264 (38.7 percent) of the total votes cast in both party primaries. The Republican candidate nominated in the primary, Stanford E. Parris, was elected to the U.S. House in the general election. The Eighth and neighboring Tenth districts, encompassing the urban suburbs of Washington, D.C., have also been the site of the only Republican legislative primaries in recent times. See table 3 in chap. 10.

Final Organization Victories

The Democrats, unlike their party foes, had no reason to forsake a system which had helped to sustain them. The string of Organization victories continued uninterrupted during the 1950s. Francis Pickens Miller locked horns with the machine once more in 1952, taking on the chieftain himself, Harry Byrd. This venture proved as unsuccessful as his first, though. In this two-way contest Miller bettered his percentage of the vote only slightly from that which he received in the four-way affair of 1949. Byrd laid to rest Miller's political ambitions by amassing 62.7 percent of the vote, and was never again to face a primary contest. For more than a decade Virginia would see no primary battle for U.S. Senate, as the anti-Organization forces finally realized the futility of challenging Byrd or Robertson under existing political conditions.[19]

Shortly after Byrd's 1952 renomination, the Democrats nominated a statewide candidate by a method other than the primary. But unlike in 1946 use of a primary would not have been possible. On September 20, 1952, Lieutenant Governor L. Preston Collins, who had been seen likely to be chosen as the next Organization candidate for governor, died suddenly of a heart attack. State law required that a vacancy in the office of the lieutenant governor was to be filled at the next succeeding general election, which at the time Collins died was only five weeks away.[20] There was clearly no time to arrange for a primary, especially in the midst of the presidential election. The Byrd primary law allowed the party to choose another method of nomination, and it was decided that the Democratic State Central Committee would undertake the task of selecting a candidate. On October 3 the committee gathered in Richmond to choose from among three candidates: state senators A. E. S. Stephens of Isle of Wight County, Edward L. Breeden, Jr., of Norfolk, and Charles R. Fenwick of Arlington (who had lost to Collins in the disputed 1945 election).[21] On the first ballot Stephens held a slim lead over Breeden and Fenwick, although no one had a majority. After another deadlocked ballot, Fenwick withdrew and threw his support to Stephens, who was then declared the nominee. Stephens was elected overwhelmingly in November over an Independent Republican even while GOP presidential nominee Dwight Eisenhower was sweeping the state and three Republicans were being elected to Congress.

---

[19] Byrd was unopposed for renomination in 1958 and 1964; Robertson was given a free primary ride in 1954 and 1960.

[20] See Code of Virginia (1950), 24-152.

[21] Richmond *Times-Dispatch,* Oct. 4, 1952.

Charles Fenwick lost a third statewide nomination in 1953 to the Organization's favorite, Thomas B. Stanley, who won the gubernatorial nomination with 65.9 percent of the primary vote. A. E. S. Stephens was renominated lieutenant governor in his first statewide primary with 75.1 percent of the vote, while incumbent machine Attorney General J. Lindsay Almond, Jr., was unopposed. Republican state Senator Ted Dalton of Radford, an able and respected legislator, threatened to defeat Stanley in the general election, but a concerted effort by the Organization produced a comfortable Democratic majority of 54.8 percent of the vote.

Controversies flared and fierce issues came and went, but, on balance, it is wondrous how little impact they seemed to have on the results of primary elections. Credit for this stability must go to the skilled leadership of the Organization and the manageable electorate which was the product of suffrage restrictions. The Massive Resistance episode in the late 1950s—when the state closed public schools in some areas rather than submit to court-ordered integration—is one excellent example of an emotion-laden issue which left deep scars on both public and politicians. Yet its impact was not felt in any major upheaval on the statewide political front which can be detected from the primary returns. The elections of 1957 and 1961 resulted in clear-cut Organization victories (although the victory margins were diminished somewhat in 1961). The 1957 primaries were notable for their lack of competition. J. Lindsay Almond, Jr.'s gubernatorial bid received an overwhelming endorsement from the voters as he garnered 79.5 percent of the vote. The Organization's nominees for lieutenant governor and attorney general, A. E. S. Stephens and Howard C. Gilmer, Jr., respectively, were unopposed. An interesting problem was presented by Gilmer, however. He withdrew before the primary under pressure, since he had been publicly associated with a questionable insurance deal, and the Organization insisted on a candidate free of any taint. However, it was too late to remove his name from the primary ballot and to substitute another candidate.[22] Gilmer declined the nomination he had won in the primary, and the Organization gave state Senator Albertis S. Harrison, Jr., its nod of approval for the attorney general's post, the Democratic State Central Committee then endorsing his nomination unanimously. A leader of the antimachine forces, Delegate

[22] An unusually large write-in vote (1,065) was recorded in the attorney general primary in 1957, a direct result of Gilmer's withdrawal. Exactly 700 votes were cast for state Senator Albertis S. Harrison, Jr., the Organization choice to succeed Gilmer. Anti-Organization leader Robert Whitehead received 283 votes, and 82 ballots were cast for others.

Robert Whitehead of Lovingston, threatened also to file and run as an Independent since there was no official Democratic primary nominee, but he later decided against such a campaign. In November, Harrison was elected overwhelmingly; his margins in cities and counties closely paralleled those of Stanley and Stephens. Apparently, the lack of a primary endorsement had little effect on the results of the general election for attorney general.

A Challenge and a Last Hurrah

Four years later in 1961 a concerted and coordinated effort by the anti-Organization forces aimed at all three top state offices also failed. Albertis Harrison won the governor's chair for the Organization with 56.7 percent of the vote in defeating antimachine convert A E. S. Stephens. State Senator Mills E. Godwin, Jr., at that time a very conservative pillar of the Organization, fended off a strong bid by state Senator Armistead L. Boothe of Alexandria to win the nomination for lieutenant governor. Godwin received 54.4 percent of the vote and a 30,000 vote majority. Finally, in the attorney general's race, Robert Y. Button defeated independent T. Munford Boyd and a third, minor candidate with a 51.9 percent majority. The election results did indicate a moderating trend among even Virginia's limited electorate. A successful Organization must always be attuned to its constituency and willing to make periodic adjustments. These qualities were evidenced in the remarkable shift of Mills Godwin from conservative to moderate during his term as lieutenant governor. With hints of major changes in state policy and a ride in 1964 on the "Lady Bird Special" campaign train through Virginia, signifying his support for Democratic presidential nominee Lyndon Johnson, Godwin was able to construct an amazing coalition of liberals, moderates, and conservatives to give the Byrd Organization one last great victory when he sought the governorship of 1965.[23] With the backing of labor, blacks, and Byrd stalwarts, Godwin and his running mates, Fred G. Pollard for lieutenant governor and incumbent Robert Y. Button as attorney general, ran unopposed in that year's Democratic primary—the first time since the primary's inception sixty years earlier that there was no contest for the nomination for any of the state's top three elective offices.[24] This

[23] For an account of this fascinating election, see Wilkinson, pp. 263-84.

[24] This feat would be repeated in 1973. The only other unopposed gubernatorial primary occurred in 1913 when Henry Carter Stuart was nominated. But there were contests for lieutenant governor and attorney general in 1913.

truly was a "last hurrah" for an Organization which had endured under two masters for the better part of a century. The strains were increasing upon, and fissures were developing in, the apparatus of the Organization, and this could be detected in the results of the general election. Defections from right and left cost Mills Godwin a majority victory, as progressive Republican Linwood Holton captured 37.7 percent of the vote and the right-wing splinter Conservative party candidate William J. Story, Jr., secured a surprising 13.4 percent.[25] Change was overtaking the machine, and this change could not be accommodated or avoided or absorbed. It struck at the very heart of the Organization, and the wound proved to be fatal. The prospects of the primary, which had prospered alongside of the machine, noticeably dimmed. Its future, if less certain than that of the Organization itself, was none too promising.

[25] The Conservative party had formed on July 10, 1965, to fight a leftward drift in the Byrd Organization. Events, such as Godwin's endorsement of President Johnson, seemed to confirm for its members a major ideological change in their former associates. Conservative candidate Story charged that because of the liberalizing trend in both major parties, the state was "slowly moving down the road to Socialistic, Communistic, Marxist control" (Richmond *News-Leader,* Oct. 1, 1965). With the electoral presence of Story and American Nazi party candidate George Lincoln Rockwell (who received 1 percent of the vote), Holton received 37.7 percent of the total vote but 44.1 percent of the two-party vote—a Republican total surpassed in recent times only by Ted Dalton in 1953.

Chapter 8

The Autumn Years of the Primary

THE 1965 general election results indicated the changes which were taking place on the political front. Within the Byrd Organization itself, there was upheaval. Older leaders, clinging to the views and policies of yesteryear, became disaffected with their younger counterparts, like Mills E. Godwin, Jr., who were beginning to respond to the new electoral realities in the Old Dominion. The path which the Organization would follow would inevitably be determined by the newer generation; age was fast overtaking the machine patriarchs. On November 11, 1965, shortly after Godwin was elected governor, Harry Flood Byrd, Sr., resigned from the U.S. Senate.[1] Incumbent Governor Albertis S. Harrison, Jr., promptly appointed Harry F. Byrd, Jr., the elder's son and a state senator from Winchester, to the vacant seat. There was more change here than met the eye, however. Granted that Byrd Jr. was basically a "faithful copy of his father,"[2] no one could really replace the aged chieftain who had ruled the Organization for almost forty years. And the many changes in suffrage restrictions and the basic structure of society which were shortly to occur combined to prevent new machine leaders from taking up where the old leaders had left off.

Restructuring Virginia's Suffrage and Representation

The reasons for the decline of the Organization, and the Democratic primary as well, will be examined in some detail in the next chapter. Suffice it to say, for now, that the roots of this decline can be found in three major legal alterations in the suffrage and the structure of representation. First, the Twenty-fourth Amendment to the U.S. Constitution, which became effective January 23, 1964, banned the poll tax or any similar tax as a prerequisite to voting in primary or general elections for federal

---

[1] Wilkinson, pp. 305-8. The timing of his announcement was not accidental. The vacancy was left to be filled by trusted lieutenant Albertis S. Harrison, Jr., rather than Godwin, whose coalitional support would bring pressure for a moderate or compromise appointee. Harry F. Byrd, Sr., died the following year.

[2] *New Republic,* Nov. 27, 1965, pp. 9-10.

offices.[3] The abolition of this tax helped to spur a registration increase of 224, 305 voters from April to October 1964, by far the greatest increase in a single election year since the State Board of Elections began collecting registration information.[4] The federal poll tax ban and subsequent registrations were a major factor in President Lyndon Johnson's Virginia victory in 1964, as he became the first Democratic presidential nominee to carry the state in sixteen years. For the first time, voter turnout in the Old Dominion topped one million, and the 41.2 percent participation by the voting age population dwarfed that of all previous Virginia elections.[5]

The Organization had realized full well the implications of the Twenty-fourth Amendment and, while ratification was still pending, had attempted to circumvent the intent of the new constitutional franchise provision. During a special session of the General Assembly in the fall of 1963, the legislature enacted a bill requiring persons who did not pay a poll tax to furnish proof of their continuing residence in the state if they planned to vote in federal elections.[6] This proof—a "certificate of residence"—was to be provided by the individual at least six months before each federal election and was to be filed with the treasurer of the city or county where the individual lived. This bill was challenged almost immediately in Richmond's federal district court, which ruled on May 29, 1964, that the legislation conflicted with the by-then-ratified Twenty-fourth Amendment and was, therefore, unconstitutional. The U.S. Supreme Court refused an appeal by the state for a stay of the decision, but eventually heard the case in 1965. In *Harman* v. *Forssenius* the Court unanimously affirmed the federal district court in striking down Virginia's "residency statute," viewing the new requirement as an "onerous procedural task

[3] The Twenty-fourth Amendment states that "the right of citizens of the United States to vote in any primary or other election for President or Vice President, for electors for President or Vice President, or for Senator or Representative in Congress, shall not be denied or abridged by the United States or any State by reason of failure to pay any poll tax or other tax" (Congressional Research Service, Library of Congress, pp. 1587-88). At the time of ratification, only five states, all southern including Virginia, still retained a poll tax. The Twenty-fourth Amendment voided the provisions of the 1902 Constitution of Virginia with respect to federal, but not state, elections.

[4] State Board of Elections, "Estimated Number of Registered Voters in Virginia, 1957 [-1964]," mimeographed (Richmond: State Board of Elections, 1957-64). Official records were not kept before April 1957, and all records for the years surveyed are compilations of estimates provided by local boards of election. About 150,000 of the voters registered between April and October 1964 did not pay any poll taxes, and consequently registered specifically to vote in federal elections.

[5] Ralph Eisenberg, "The 1964 Presidential Election in Virginia: A Political Omen?" *University of Virginia News Letter* 41 (April 15, 1965): 29-32. Johnson received 53.5 percent of the vote.

[6] *Acts of the Assembly, Extra Session, 1963,* c. 2, pp. 4-9.

which unquestionably erects a real obstacle to voting in federal elections for those who assert their constitutional exemption from the poll tax" and was therefore an unconstitutional "abridgement" of that exemption.[7] It was only a matter of time before the poll tax ban was extended to state elections. A little more than a year after the ratification of the Twenty-fourth Amendment, the U.S. Congress had passed at President Johnson's initiative the Voting Rights Act of 1965, which included a clause forbidding collection of the poll tax as a voting qualification in state elections.[8] In 1966 the U.S. Supreme Court voided the last vestiges of the poll tax in a Virginia case, *Harper* v. *Virginia State Board of Elections,* ruling that the tax was a clear violation of the equal protection clause of the Fourteenth Amendment.[9]

The second set of legal decisions which restructured Virginia politics concerned legislative apportionment. Beginning with a Tennessee case, *Baker* v. *Carr,* in 1962, the Supreme Court began to require that representation be allotted on an equal population basis so that the weight of each individual's vote would be equal.[10] The Court applied its "one man, one vote" principle to congressional districting in 1964[11] and later that same year issued a decision which rocked the foundations of state capitols throughout the country. In *Reynolds* v. *Sims* an emphatic Court interpreted the Fourteenth Amendment's equal protection clause to require that both houses of a bicameral state legislature be apportioned by population.[12] Chief Justice Earl Warren insisted that "legislators represent

[7] 380 U.S. 528, 541 (1965). See also Congressional Research Service, Library of Congress, p. 1588.

[8] Voting Rights Act of 1965, §10.79 Stat. 442, 42 U.S.C. §1973h. For the results of actions instituted by the attorney general of the United States under direction of their section, see *United States* v. *Texas* 252 F. Supp. 234 (D.C.W.D. Tex. 1966) (three-judge court) affirmed on other grounds, 384 U.S. 155 (1966); and *United States* v. *Alabama,* 252 F. Supp. 95 (D.C.M.D. Ala. 1966) (three-judge court).

[9] 383 U.S. 663 (1966). The timing of these court and congressional actions, however, enabled Virginia to conduct the 1965 gubernatorial election with the poll tax provisions intact. As the last election in the Old Dominion under the requirement which had sustained the Organization for 60 years, the 1965 primary is an appropriate point to mark the end of the machine era and the beginning of a new political day in Virginia.

[10] *Baker* v. *Carr,* 369 U.S. 186 (1962). For an excellent discussion of legislative apportionment and the effects of court-ordered redistricting in the United States, see Thomas R. Dye, "State Legislative Politics" in Herbert Jacob and Kenneth N. Vines, eds., *Politics in the American States: A Comparative Analysis* (2d ed., Boston: Little, Brown, and Company, 1971), pp. 169-76.

[11] *Wesberry* v. *Saunders,* 376 U.S. 1 (1964).

[12] *Reynolds* v. *Sims,* 377 U.S. 533, 562 (1964). The reader is also referred to two other major reapportionment cases heard by the Supreme Court: *Colegrove* v. *Green,* 328 U.S. 549 (1946), which illustrates the "hands off" stance which the Supreme Court took for

people, not trees or acres," although many legislators in Virginia and across the nation seemed to disagree. Faced with the Court edict, the General Assembly met in 1964 and transferred eleven seats from rural to urban areas.[13] Further, the Assembly was forced to hold a special election for all state Senate seats in the 1965 Democratic primary and general election.[14] Even more important than the initial gains for urban areas, however, was the promise of greater future urban and suburban representation, since the population was expanding rapidly in those areas of Virginia. The Organization, heavily based in rural Southside and other non-urban areas, thus was substantially weakened in the representative body most important to its continued survival and success—the General Assembly.

A third development in the middle 1960s resulted in the addition of many more thousands of black Virginians to the voting rolls. The Voting Rights Act, passed in August 1965, banned literacy tests and similar devices in states where less than 50 percent of the eligible voting population was registered or had cast ballots in the 1964 presidential election. Virginia and five other southern states fell under that ban.[15] The act authorized federal registrars to enter these states, if necessary, to enforce its provisions. Additionally, affected states and localities were required to submit any changes in election law or districts for federal approval. Observers in Virginia have agreed, for the most part, that the Voting Rights Act helped to register thousands of the state's black citizens and removed many voting impediments used on a local level by registrars.[16] The Virginia electorate no longer bore any resemblance to a "great party of white friends," and the results of primary elections began to reflect this.

many years; and *Gray* v. *Sanders,* 372 U.S. 368 (1963), which abolished the county unit system of voting and eloquently expressed the Court's newfound reapportionment philosophy.

[13] Wilkinson, p. 249. Virginia's underrepresentation of urban areas was not so severe as in some states. For a comparative analysis, see Paul T. David and Ralph Eisenberg, *Devaluation of the Urban and Suburban Vote* (Charlottesville: Bureau of Public Administration, University of Virginia, 1961).

[14] See State Board of Elections, *Statement of the Vote Cast for Members of the Senate and the House of Delegates in the General Election Held November 2, 1965* (Richmond: Department of Purchases and Supply, 1965).

[15] Forty counties in North Carolina also came under the provisions of the act. Counties in ten additional states came under the act after its 1970 extension.

[16] See Margaret Scott, "Voting Rights Act Nears Its 10th Year," Norfolk *Virginian-Pilot,* July 13, 1975, pp. C-1 to C-2. This lengthy article contains a perceptive analysis of the effects of the Voting Rights Act and is supplemented by an account of the changes which have taken place as a result of the act in Brunswick County, in the heart of the old Organization's Southside.

In rapid-fire fashion, then, the restricted electorate which had been made-to-order for a political machine by the 1901-2 Constitutional Convention was transformed. The phenomenon of urbanization complemented the abolition of the poll tax, the reapportionment of legislative districts, and the enrollment of blacks to bring a new political order to the Commonwealth. As the next chapter will explain, the causes of the recent success of the Republican party and the realignment of state parties to conform with their national counterparts—not to mention the decline of the primary—can be traced to these developments.

The Primary Reflects the Change

After 1966 Virginia politics were described in new terms. Where the Old Dominion's elections had been called "predictable and orderly," electoral trends were now seen as "tumultuous and confused." The Democratic primaries for U.S. Senate in 1966 illustrate the contrast.[17] Harry F. Byrd, Jr., newly appointed to his father's seat, faced a primary challenge from state Senator Armistead L. Boothe of Alexandria, a longtime foe of the Organization. A. Willis Robertson, then completing his third full term, was opposed by state Senator William B. Spong, Jr., of Portsmouth, who had been a quieter member of the anti-Organization faction. Virginia Democrats had not had a primary for a U.S. Senate seat since 1952, but the opponents of the Organization were encouraged to make the race by the legal developments just reviewed. Spong and Boothe's analysis was accurate, even though only one of them won in the primary election. By the narrowest of margins (50.1 percent of the vote), Spong unseated Robertson, while Byrd barely survived his challenger, winning but 50.9 percent of the vote. In an even greater shock to the Organization, U.S Representative Howard W. Smith was defeated for renomination to the seat he had held since 1931 by liberal George C. Rawlings, Jr., of Fredericksburg. Rawlings's victory was also a narrow one, just 50.6 percent of

[17] For only the second time since the adoption of the primary system, Virginians were able to select nominees for both U.S. Senate seats. Four years remained in the term of Byrd, Sr., while Robertson's term regularly expired in 1966. The other double Senate election had occurred in 1911. Two senators were also elected in 1946, but only one (Byrd) was nominated in a primary, while the other (Robertson) was selected by a convention.

For this and subsequent elections, the reader is referred to a series of articles by Ralph Eisenberg, as noted in the bibliography, which discuss elections in the Old Dominion during the 1960s, and to my *Virginia Votes, 1969-1974* (Charlottesville: Institute of Government, University of Virginia, 1976), which provides an analysis of the most recent national, state, and congressional district elections in Virginia.

the total vote. Although the margins of the triumphant antimachine candidates were small, they had defeated the Organization in an all-out battle, something no one else had done in a primary since Westmoreland Davis in the complicated three-way gubernatorial race of 1917.[18] One did not have to look beyond the record primary turnout of 434,217 or the votes cast by blacks and urban areas to explain this novel result. Spong and Byrd defeated two relatively unknown Republican opponents comfortably, but not overwhelmingly, in November.[19]

The collapse of the primary came as a direct result of the statewide election of 1969. The battle to succeed Mills Godwin as governor became a three-way contest with each ideological faction of the Democratic party represented. William C. Battle of Charlottesville, son of former Organization governor John Battle and the campaign manager for Spong in the 1966 primary, had the support of moderate party members and some Organization men. The greater part of the Organization, however, was allied with Lieutenant Governor Fred G. Pollard of Richmond. Liberals and many traditional anti-Organization supporters rallied behind state Senator Henry E. Howell, Jr., of Norfolk. Fierce contests also developed for the posts of lieutenant governor and attorney general. State senators J. Sargeant Reynolds of Richmond, a moderate-liberal, and Carrington Thompson of Pittsylvania County, an Organization-conservative and a member of Pollard's ticket, were the main contenders for the state's second post.[20] Another moderate, Andrew P. Miller, sought the attorney

[18] Some might contend that Glass in 1920 or Price in 1937 had been able to defeat the Organization. While this may be true in one sense—it was their strength or popularity which caused the Organization to accommodate them—neither won in the face of strong and open opposition from the Organization. It cannot be said for sure that they could have been elected against such opposition. Before 1917 the Organization was defeated in an occasional congressional contest, such as those involving Jones or Glass. After 1917, however, it was not beaten in a single major primary contest, although a few Republicans won seats in the U.S. House of Representatives in the general elections.
[19] See Ralph Eisenberg, "1966 Politics in Virginia: The Elections for U.S. Senators," *University of Virginia News Letter* 43 (May 15, 1967): 33–36, and Eisenberg, "1966 Politics in Virginia: The Elections for U.S. Representatives," ibid., 43 (June 15, 1967): 37–40.
Spong won 58.6 percent of the vote to 33.5 percent for Republican James P. Ould, Jr., and 7.9 percent for Conservative F. Lee Hawthorne. Byrd did less well than Spong, receiving only 53.3 percent of the vote. His opponents, Republican Lawrence M. Traylor, Conservative John W. Carter, and Independent J. B. Brayman, won 37.4, 7.9, and 1.4 percent, respectively.
[20] Other candidates were Herman "Hardtimes" Hunt and Moses A. Riddick, Jr. Only twice before had so many candidates run in a primary for a single post. The attorney general's race had an equally large field.

general nomination, opposed by Delegate Guy O. Farley, Jr., of Fairfax County and two other candidates.[21]

The campaign was more expensive, and perhaps more vigorous and bitter, than any in Virginia's primary history. When it was over, Battle had secured a small plurality victory of 38.9 percent over Howell, who received 37.8 percent of the vote. Organization candidate Pollard was far out of the running with only 23.3 percent of the total. Virginia's first (and only) runoff under the 1952 statute would finally be held, both for governor and attorney general. Andrew Miller had won his contest but had not amassed a majority.[22] Only J. Sargeant Reynolds was able to avoid a runoff by winning his race with a vote of landslide proportions (63.9 percent).

The second primary was even more bitter than the first. Battle emerged the victor, but by the relatively slim margin of 52.1 percent to 47.9 percent for Howell. Miller scored an impressive victory in his race by taking 63.2 percent of the vote. A large black and urban vote had increased Miller's total and, at the same time, almost resulted in a victory for Howell.[23] In the 1969 primaries, then, all of the Organization's candidates had been soundly defeated. While some elements of the Organization supported Battle, especially in the runoff primary, they were only one of many components of the Battle vote. The 1969 Democratic primary confirmed that control of the party's nomination had passed from the machine's hands.

In November it became obvious as well that control of elective offices in Virginia had passed from the hands of the Democratic party. Republican Linwood Holton of Roanoke defeated Battle by a solid majority (52.5 percent) in taking hold of the governorship for his party for the first time since the 1880s.[24] Urban and black votes again made the difference, as Holton benefited from the Democratic disaffection of many Howell supporters. In their first Republican "fling" in connection with state office, more than a few Organization voters also cast a ballot for Holton.[25] Conservative Democrats, no longer calling the shots in party

[21] Other candidates were Delegate Bernard Levin of Norfolk and C. F. "Flip" Hicks. Delegate Farley was also a member of Pollard's ticket.

[22] Miller received 41.2 percent to 35.0 percent for Farley, 12.7 percent for Levin, and 11.1 percent for Hicks.

[23] For an analysis of the election returns, see Ralph Eisenberg, "1969 Politics in Virginia: The Democratic Party Primary," *University of Virginia News Letter* 46 (Feb. 15, 1970): 21–24, and Sabato, *Virginia Votes*, section 1.

[24] Battle received 45.4 percent, and minor candidates accounted for the difference. William E. Cameron, governor from 1882 to 1888, was technically a "readjuster Republican"; see Moger, pp. 37–39.

[25] See Eisenberg, "1969 Politics in Virginia: The General Election," *University of Virginia News Letter* 46 (May 15, 1970): 33–36, and Sabato, *Virginia Votes*, section 1. Of

or primary, were deserting the house of their fathers. Democrats Reynolds and Miller, however, were able to contain the defections and were elected to the posts of lieutenant governor and attorney general.

The Loyalty Oath Revisited

The ferment within the Democratic party was apparent as a new decade dawned. Moderate and liberal Democrats already formed an electoral majority, and their eyes turned toward the upcoming primary for the Senate seat of Harry F. Byrd, Jr. The new reality within the party also required new rules, and on February 21, 1970, the Democratic State Central Committee adopted some bylaws to the party plan. Certainly with the problems of 1969 party defectors in mind, the committee revised the loyalty oath, exempting voters from its provisions and making it applicable to candidates only. For the candidates, however, it was tightened to negate the 1929 opinion of Attorney General John Saunders. Party loyalty would now include support of presidential electors.[26] A subcommittee was formed to study and revise the entire party plan, and its members were instructed to consider complete abolition of the loyalty oath for candidates as well as voters. But for the 1970 primary election at least the broadened loyalty oath would apply.

On March 17 Senator Byrd announced that he could not and would not subscribe to the revised loyalty oath, since it would bind him to support the 1972 Democratic presidential ticket. Therefore, he would skip the party primary and run for reelection as an Independent Democrat in November. (The emphasis on "Democrat" was later dropped.) Byrd's only public reason for his decision was the loyalty oath: "I am told that I could sign such an oath and forget it. Perhaps there is a technicality behind which I could hide, but the intent of the committee requirement is clear. Whatever I do, I want to do in good faith." Yet, it was publicly clear by then that the Democrats would probably abolish the loyalty oath in several weeks. Should that occur, the oath Byrd would take would apply only to the election of 1970. This suggests that a major factor in Byrd's decision was

course, many machine-oriented Democrats had been casting GOP ballots in presidential elections for years.

[26] Richmond *Times-Dispatch*, Feb. 22, 1970. Exact wording of the broadened party loyalty oath was as follows: "I, . . ., of . . ., Virginia, do state on my sacred honor that I am a member of the Democratic party and believe in its principles, that I shall support and vote for all of the nominees of said party, including those for presidential elector, if any, chosen by the state Democratic convention in Virginia, at the next ensuing general election."

to avoid the primary itself. A poll taken for Byrd indicated that he would have a much more difficult time being renominated than in being reelected.[27] The reason for this could be found in the different compositions of the primary and general electorates. Blacks, liberals, and urban individuals would constitute a greater part of the electorate in the primary than in the November election which followed. This phenomenon will receive greater attention in the succeeding chapter.

On May 2, 1970, Democrats abandoned their party loyalty oath entirely and the mandatory statewide primary as well. These astounding developments were the product of labors by the party's resolutions and steering committee appointed earlier and were adopted by the full 110-member state central committee in session at the Hotel Roanoke, the old sanctuary-in-exile of the Virginia GOP during its lean years. The new party plan required of members only that they "believe in the principles of the Democratic party." One additional provision was added unanimously as a compromise to which all factions had agreed: "No person shall participate as a candidate in any Democratic primary election nor as a candidate or otherwise in a convention or mass meeting, who intends to support any candidate opposed to a Democratic nominee in the next ensuing general election." While this arrangement would apply to presidential electors, it gives a tacit approval of "golden silences" and is more of an "antidisloyalty oath," as political columnist Charles McDowell called it. No longer did one pledge on his sacred honor that present, past, and future nominees had been supported, only that they had not been opposed. The revised party plan did call for an increased loyalty on the part of party officials on the local level. Democratic committees were ordered to "remove from both office and membership any person who shall be guilty of willful neglect of any duty imposed upon him or of supporting for any office, for which a nominee of the Democratic party has been certified, the nominee of any other political party, including presidential electors, or any independent candidate." This latter clause would be applicable during the 1970 Senate contest, and would cause numerous party resignations of Byrd-oriented officials. Some weighty alterations had been made, and the new legalisms of party membership could make humorous reading, as McDowell surmised: "The new rules . . . define a Democrat roughly as anyone who thinks he is. Members of Democratic committees are required to demonstrate at least a polite proclivity for Democratic candidates. As for candidates, they cannot run in a Democratic primary if they 'intend' to support anybody other than the winner of the primary. Presumably, a candidate could maintain a 'golden silence' . . . or he could change his

[27] Richmond *Times-Dispatch*, Mar. 18, 1970.

intent at the last minute . . . without injuring his status as a Democrat. By one interpretation, a man sound asleep, his mind free of intent, automatically would be a Democrat."[28]

The mandatory primary in Virginia also was relegated to the history books by the 1970 party plan. Primaries for U.S. senator, governor, lieutenant governor, and attorney general would henceforth be optional, to be determined each year by the state central committee. Party officers, in their comments in and out of the meeting, made clear that this change was a reaction to the 1969 primaries. As in the old plan, the appropriate party committee would determine the method of nomination for congressmen, legislators, and local officials. In past years these decisions had almost always resulted in primary elections in most regions of Virginia. It was apparent that future decisions would not be so predictable.

These institutional blows suffered by the primary were not nearly as serious as the wound inflicted on July 14, 1970. For all of the controversy and political machinations which had surrounded it, voters did not appear particularly interested in the Democratic primary for U.S. Senate. A paltry 129,959 voters went to the polls; dozens of precincts throughout the state reported not a single vote cast. The vote represented a 70 percent decline from the 1969 runoff, and the total participation was much lower than most elections during the era of suffrage restrictions. Liberal George C. Rawlings, Jr., of Fredericksburg, who had beaten Congressman Smith in the 1966 primary only to be defeated in November by a Republican, won a narrow plurality victory of 45.7 percent over his moderate opponent, Delegate Clive DuVal II of Fairfax, who received 45.1 percent. A relatively unknown college professor, Milton Colvin, accounted for slightly under 10 percent of the vote. Earlier in the year the General Assembly had abolished the runoff primary provisions (no doubt with the 1969 experience in mind), but the new code did not take effect until December.[29] Legally, then, another runoff election was possible in 1970. But earlier all three primary candidates had signed a formal agreement with the Democratic State Central Committee not to request a runoff if they were later in a position to do so.[30] One "escape clause" in this agreement, however, permitted a runoff request if the difference between the two top candidates was less than one percent of the vote—a situation

[28] Richmond *Times-Dispatch,* May 3, 1970.

[29] The legislature also abolished at this time any statutory mention of the party loyalty oath or of provisions for challenge of voters at the polls. This left the matter entirely to party rules under a section of the Byrd primary law. This legislative action was taken in tandem with the party's reconsideration of its plan, and was designed to facilitate any challenges which the party might decide to make.

[30] Richmond *Times-Dispatch*, July 15, 1970.

which did indeed exist in 1970. There was some considerable feeling that DuVal could win the runoff,[31] but he waived his right to a second primary. In light of the turnout, he may have felt that the nomination was not worth the additional effort, and it would also be hard to justify the expense to both public treasury and party health of another election. DuVal may actually have had the better of it in this first "year of the Independent." Harry F. Byrd, Jr., swept to an easy victory over Rawlings and Republican Ray Garland, who had been nominated by convention. Byrd secured a majority of 53.5 percent in the three-way contest, leaving Rawlings and Garland to split the remainder of the vote.[32] A Byrd had been reelected in Virginia—an event which would hardly make newspaper headlines throughout the country. But this Byrd in this year owed his election not to the Organization of old nor to a newly constructed one. Rather, the issues Byrd raised, complemented by well-financed media and get-out-the-vote efforts, were really responsible for his victory.

The Democratic experience of 1970 had some party officials publicly suggesting that the time had come for the party to turn to nominating conventions.[33] Yet the primary still had its advocates within the party. Some individuals, like state Senator Henry Howell, felt threatened by a convention which might be controlled by political adversaries. Howell and others sponsored a successful amendment to the primary law in 1970, which stated in part: "No party which at the immediately preceding election for a particular office nominated its candidate for such office by a primary, and such nominee was elected at the general election, shall choose to nominate a candidate for the next election for such office by any method other than by a primary, without the consent of the incumbent." This clause has been invoked on numerous occasions at every elective level since its adoption.[34] One further change in the statutes was

---

[31] This deduction was based on the assumption that conservative Milton Colvin's voters would be more inclined to support moderate DuVal than liberal Rawlings. Such presumptions are shaky, of course, as DuVal undoubtedly realized. Assuming that Colvin's voters would participate in a second primary, it did not necessarily follow that they would support DuVal. The 1969 runoff illustrates that "ideological logic" is not a good electoral yardstick. The aggregate statistics in cities and counties for the 1969 gubernatorial primary and runoff elections strongly suggest that liberal Henry Howell in the runoff received a good portion of the votes first cast for conservative Fred Pollard.

[32] Rawlings received 31.2 percent, and Garland only 15.3 percent of the vote.

[33] Almost as soon as the 1970 primary election votes were totaled, state Senator William B. Hopkins of Roanoke, a Democratic national committeeman, began advocating the convention method of nomination (Richmond *Times-Dispatch*, July 15, 1970).

[34] *Acts of the Assembly, 1970*, c. 462, p. 867. U.S. Senator William B. Spong, Jr., utilized it in 1972, as did Andrew P. Miller in his 1973 renomination bid for attorney general.

made in 1970 to assist the primary in its fight for survival. The date of the primary election was moved from July to the second Tuesday in June (effective in 1971),[35] to give party candidates longer to prepare for the general election battle with a strengthened Republican party, and perhaps also to allow more time for the bitterness generated by many primary contests to fade.

A Convention in 1971

Just as they had done in 1946, Democratic officials used legal technicalities to support their decision to hold a party convention rather than a primary to fill a vacancy in 1971. Youthful Lieutenant Governor J. Sargeant Reynolds died in early June of complications arising from a brain tumor. Normally, the deadline for holding a primary would have long since passed, but a legislative redistricting battle had resulted in a court-ordered postponement of the primaries until September 14. It was still possible, then, for the eleven-member Democratic state steering committee to arrange for a primary when they met on June 16.[36] Instead, the committee voted down the primary on a 7-to-3 roll call, with only the Tidewater and Northern Virginia representatives supporting the Democrats' traditional method of nomination. The 118-member state central committee then had the option of selecting a candidate itself or holding a convention. It chose the latter, and so the first statewide Democratic nominating convention since 1946 was scheduled to be held August 14 in Hampton. Party officials again cited the divisiveness and expense of the 1969 gubernatorial primary in explaining their decision. There was no dearth of candidates in the convention, as five individuals formally announced and almost a dozen other Democrats maneuvered behind the scenes for supports.[37] The major battle developed between liberal Delegate Carrington Williams of Fairfax and moderate-conservative Delegate George J. Kostel of Clifton Forge. On the fourth ballot, Kostel emerged victorious as he gained a majority of the convention ballots.[38] Meanwhile, Republicans had followed their normal nominating procedure to select

[35] Ibid.

[36] The committee met exactly 90 days from the scheduled date of the primaries, which is the deadline provided by law for the calling of a primary election.

[37] Richmond *Times-Dispatch*, June 17, July 3–Aug. 14, 1971.

[38] Other major candidates included four conservatives: Delegate D. French Slaughter, Jr., of Culpeper, Delegate George N. McMath of the Eastern Shore, Senator Robert C. Fitzgerald of Fairfax, and Senator Hunter B. Andrews of Hampton. The final ballot showed 784 votes for Kostel, 730 for Williams, and 42 for Fitzgerald (Richmond *Times-Dispatch*, Aug. 15, 1971).

Delegate George P. Shafran of Arlington, a favorite of Governor Holton, by convention. The ultimate victor, as in 1970, was nominated by neither party. State Senator Henry Howell, protesting the Democratic decision to drop the primary, announced his Independent candidacy. It was a plurality victory for Howell in November, as the liberal Independent garnered 40 percent of the vote. Democrat Kostel was not far behind with 36.9 percent, while the Republican candidate trailed badly for the second consecutive year.

Party Realignment

In 1952 political scientist Alexander Heard predicted what he saw as an inevitable realignment of the two parties in Virginia. Because of social and economic developments the southern Democratic party would gradually liberalize, alienating conservatives. Third-party or independent movements, Heard suggested, were usually failures. "In the long run southern conservatives will find neither in a separatist group nor in the Democratic party an adequate vehicle of political expression. If this is true, they must turn to the Republican party."[39] In 1972 Heard's prediction came to pass in the Old Dominion. The liberal wing, aided by "full-participation" rules adopted by the national party, seized control of the state Democratic party. Joseph T. Fitzpatrick of Norfolk was elected state party chairman, and George C. Rawlings, Jr., of Fredericksburg and Ruth Harvey Charity of Danville became Virginia's representatives on the national party committee. All three replaced moderates, and all were associated with liberal Henry Howell. As the pendulum swung left in the state Democratic party, it swung right in Virginia's GOP. Moderate Holton Republicans were ousted from party leadership positions, as conservative Richard Obenshain took the party helm. For the first time in the post–Civil War history of the Commonwealth, the state parties were comfortable and aligned with their national counterparts. The upheaval in the parties did not affect the nomination of U.S. Senator William B. Spong, Jr., since he was unopposed in the primary—a primary which he had requested under the provisions of the 1970 incumbent's act discussed earlier. But in November the effects of party realignments became clearer, as the moderate Spong was upset by conservative Republican William L. Scott of Fairfax. Scott defeated Spong by almost 75,000 votes.[40]

[39] Alexander Heard, *A Two-Party South?* (Chapel Hill: University of North Carolina Press, 1952), p. 247.

[40] The percentages were: Scott, 51.5; Spong, 46.1; Independent Horace "Hunk" Henderson of Virginia Beach, 2.43.

The Democratic party, if not the primary, reached its nadir in 1973. For the first time since Reconstruction the party had no gubernatorial candidate, as no one filed for the primary.[41] Andrew P. Miller was unopposed for renomination to the attorney general's post, and state Senator J. Harry Michael of Charlottesville received the party nod for lieutenant governor without opposition. Citing a lack of money and organization, Michael publicly indicated that he would not run for the post if he was to be opposed in the primary. He was permitted a free primary ride, but even this gesture of party unity did not help him in November, as he was defeated by a Republican, state Senator John N. Dalton of Radford, adopted son of "Mr. Republican" Ted Dalton. Another Republican candidate, former Democratic governor Mills E. Godwin, Jr., narrowly defeated Independent Lieutenant Governor Henry Howell in the governor's contest. Miller won easily in his race, becoming the only Democratic statewide candidate to be elected in four years.[42]

More Changes in Party Rules

The loyalty oath controversy surfaced once more in 1973. On June 10, with the remaining moderate and conservative members of the Democratic State Central Committee opposed, the committee adopted on a vote of 65 to 45 the following addition to the party plan:

No Democratic committee member or officer of any Democratic Committee shall publicly support, endorse or assist the duly nominated candidates of another political party. In the event any Democratic Committee member or officer of any Democratic Committee shall undertake such public activities, the appropriate Democratic Committee shall remove said person from office. Such action shall not be taken without notice to the offending member and an opportunity for him to refute such charges. In the event that no action is taken against such person, the Congressional District Committee shall initiate the necessary action in lieu thereof. The Steering Committee of the Democratic State Central Committee may take further action within thirty (30) days after the receipt of

[41] The record of Independent Henry Howell was "commended," but the candidate himself was not officially endorsed or nominated by the party's central committee. The liberals who had gained control of the party in 1972 were considered friends of the primary nomination method. Had there been a gubernatorial contest, it is likely that a primary would have been chosen to nominate the candidate.

[42] Percentages are as follows: governor: Godwin, 50.7, Howell, 49.3; lieutenant governor: Dalton, 54.0, Michael, 35.5, Independent Flora Crater, 10.5; attorney general: Miller, 70.6, Republican M. Patton Echols, Jr., 29.4. See Sabato, *Aftermath of Armageddon: An Analysis of the 1973 Gubernatorial Election* (Charlottesville: Institute of Government, University of Virginia, 1975).

a written complaint by any member of the Democratic Party in relation to such matters. . . . The obligations imposed on [local party] committees and their members by [the above provisions] shall not be deemed to require support of any candidate who is himself publicly supporting a nominee on the ticket of any other political party in any General Election where Democratic candidates for office appear on the ballot, or who publicly supports any other candidate opposed to a Democratic nominee.[43]

This new approach to the party loyalty issue was a novel one, since it applied, not to voters or candidates, but to party officers alone. It was designed, in part, to help Howell's gubernatorial candidacy, as was a resolution passed by the central committee on the same day "commending" Howell to the voters. Even though the Organization ruled they had insisted on a binding loyalty pledge, conservatives were rankled by the new language. Watkins Abbitt, a former Organization congressman and chairman of the Democrats for Godwin Committee, attacked the provision as "onerous" and "yet another tangible demonstration of the vicious McGovern wing of the party in Virginia . . . impos[ing] its will on the party." Godwin himself called the oath "tyrannical and punitive."[44] The results of the new oath were less earthshaking than the rhetoric which surrounded its adoption. There were scattered resignations from Democratic committees but few apparent challenges of personnel within the party's local and district organs. The provisions survived later revisions of the party plan and were adopted anew in 1975. In the latter year a loyalty clause of sorts was reinstituted for primary voters and participants in Democratic mass meetings and conventions. It closely resembled the "antidisloyalty oath" adopted for candidates in 1970, forbidding a primary or convention vote to anyone "who intends to support a candidate or candidates opposed to any Democratic nominee" in the general election. Further, a new "challenge" provision was added in 1975, providing that an individual voter who is challenged in a primary on grounds that he is not a Democrat must state verbally in the presence of two or more election officials that he is a Democrat and does not intend to support any candidate opposed to a Democratic nominee in the ensuing general or special election.[45] An election law amendment passed by the General Assembly in 1976, however, negates the challenge provision. Conservative House majority leader James Thomson of Alexandria, fearing that some of his supporters might be barred from the primary polling booth, success-

---

[43] Democratic Party Plan as amended June 10, 1973, Article XIII, sections 9 and 10.
[44] Richmond *Times-Dispatch*, June 11, June 12, June 14, 1973.
[45] Democratic Party Plan, 1975, Article II, section 2, and Article XXVII, section 4.

fully and quietly steered the amendment to passage in both houses—to the eventual and belated dismay of Democratic party loyalists and liberals.[46]

Nowhere can the decline of the primary be seen more clearly than in the region of its strongest support within the Democratic party. Since the 1972 liberal takeover of the party apparatus, Northern Virginia representatives had repeatedly attempted to reestablish the mandatory primary at the statewide level, and perhaps the congressional district level as well. These efforts had been staunchly and successfully opposed by the Southwest Virginia region and other areas. In 1974 only two congressional districts, the Northern Virginia Eighth and Tenth, held primaries. The turnout in both district elections was dismal, despite active campaigns and a multicandidate field in each district. Of 178,000 registered voters in the Eighth, only 14,400 individuals voted (8.1 percent), and the neighboring Tenth could boast only a slightly better (11.2 percent) turnout of the registered electorate.[47] These participation rates did little to recommend the primary method to other parts of the state. The primary in the Tenth District actually provided party leaders with another reason to avoid the primary nomination method. Dennis Gregg, a young and unconventional congressional candidate, was allowed to file for the primary election without the traditional payment of an $850 fee. Despite unencumbered assets totaling thousands of dollars, Gregg pleaded his financial inability to pay the fee to the State Board of Elections, which in turn sought a formal opinion from Attorney General Andrew Miller. That opinion construed a recent decision by the U.S. Supreme Court in a California case to mean that, unless it provides a reasonable alternative for access to the ballot, a state may not require filing fees from an indigent candidate. The attorney general further opined that, in Virginia, opportunity to seek office as an independent did not constitute a reasonable alternative for ballot access, thus leading to the conclusion that Virginia's filing fee requirement was "invalid as applied to an indigent candidate who affirmatively demonstrates that he is unable to pay the assessed fee." The net result of the Gregg decision by the State Board of Elections was to discourage primaries further. Many Democratic officials feared that future primary elections would now be open to numerous "nuisance" candidates with less than serious motives.[48]

[46] See James Latimer, "Primary Law Change Criticized by Howell," Richmond *Times-Dispatch*, April 7, 1976, p. A-1.

[47] Turnout in terms of the potential vote (population aged 18 years or older) was even drearier. Only 3.1 percent of the potential vote in the Eighth, and 5.5 percent in the Tenth, cast a ballot in the 1974 primary election.

[48] *Opinions of the Attorney General and Report to the Governor, 1973–74*, pp. 153–54; *Lubin v. Panish*, 415 U.S. 709 (1974); Richmond *Times-Dispatch*, April 24, 28, 1974.

A complex series of events which began with Harry Byrd, Sr.'s resignation and ended with the barren primary election of 1974 has now been reviewed. The abolition of the poll tax on state and federal levels, reapportionment of the state legislature and congressional districts, and enrollment of large numbers of black citizens combined with the explosive growth of urban and suburban areas to forge a new political reality in the Old Dominion during the late 1960s and early 1970s. Part of that new reality was the decline of the Democratic party primary. The reasons for this decline are examined in more detail in the chapter which follows.

Chapter 9

An Examination of the Primary's Decline

THROUGHOUT this study fragmented explanations for the rise and fall of the primary system in Virginia have appeared. It is this chapter's purpose to attempt a more comprehensive review of the reasons for the primary's decline and to develop a general theory of the relationship between primary and interparty competition in Virginia. The causal factors which will be discussed are all interrelated. Indeed, their multicollinearity makes any real assessment of causality hazardous at best. This task is perhaps akin to that of unraveling the Gordian knot; yet despite the admitted difficulties involved, a reasonable and logical progression of developments can be formulated to account for the Virginia experience with the direct primary.

The Primary's Effect on the GOP

Basic to this discussion is the premise that the institution of the Democratic primary in Virginia helped to engineer the decline of the state's Republican party.[1] To offer evidence of this result, one must first look beyond the machinations of Organization and anti-Organization maneuverings to the basic need which gave rise to the direct primary in Virginia and throughout the nation: "The direct primary method of nomination apparently constituted at bottom an escape from one-partyism. . . . With the states of the South irrevocably tied to the Democratic party and with many of the states of the North and West almost equally attached to the Republican party, oligarchical control of party—of which the nominating convention became the symbol and often the reality— amounted to a denial of popular government."[2]

[1] This discussion will rely heavily on the thoughts of V. O. Key in *Southern Politics*, pp. 298–311. Many of Key's ideas are expanded throughout Alexander Heard, *A Two-Party South?* and summary of the basic concepts proposed by Key and Heard is presented by Wilkinson, pp. 199–208. The reader is also referred to the arguments of Austin Ranney concerning the doctrine of responsible party government as it relates to the direct primary, contained throughout *The Doctrine of Responsible Party Government*.

[2] Key, *American State Politics*, p. 88. Key offers much evidence to support his contention by examining both the chronological pattern of the adoption of the direct primary by the states and the comprehensiveness of the primary systems in the states. See pp. 89–92.

The primary was necessary, then, to correct the evils of a one-party system. This need was also basic in Virginia after the adoption of the Constitution of 1902. Before the new Constitution's suffrage restrictions eliminated a large number of Republican voters, the GOP in Virginia did provide a measure of competition for the Democrats in statewide races and certainly in many specific regions of the Commonwealth, and this competition could well have been a factor in the state's delay in adopting the primary.

Apart from the suffrage restrictions, the Republican party was further weakened by the direct primary itself. The focus of electoral decision and the voter's concern shifted from the general election, where the Republican party was one of two main actors, to the primary, where two or more intraparty factions shared the stage and spotlight. "Voters [may be] attracted to the primary of one party and there fight out the issues that would otherwise be settled in the general election campaign, with the result that whatever consistency of attitude party candidates might otherwise have over a period of time is broken. In the process the minority party may be weakened or virtually destroyed."[3] Thus, a major result of the institution of the direct primary is the substitution of intraparty politics for interparty politics. Factions form within the dominant party, which can be of a transitory or semipermanent nature. In Virginia, more so than any other southern state, the factions became semipermanent.[4] They organized themselves and functioned in a manner not dissimilar from that of political parties as we normally conceive them—although some important differences do exist, as will be discussed shortly. Other states south of the Mason-Dixon line had factions much less clearly defined and more oriented to individual personalities than Virginia.

Key introduced a political axiom which can certainly be applied to the relationship between Democratic primary and Republican party: "Institutional decay follows deprivation of function."[5] The direct primary removed the monopoly of electoral opposition enjoyed by the GOP in Virginia. Although the suffrage restrictions had a damaging effect on the party's membership base, the primary is at least as responsible for the atrophy of the state GOP because of the devastating effect which it had on leadership recruitment. The abilities and vision of a party's leaders

---

[3] Key, *Politics, Parties, and Pressure Groups*, p. 387.
[4] Some statistical data will be presented in chap. 10 which support this contention. Key in *Southern Politics*, pp. 17–19, also concluded that such a situation existed in Virginia.
[5] Key, *American State Politics*, p. 195.

are crucial to its development and prosperity; this factor is often under-estimated in an examination of a party's decline. The primary, in effect, drew the best potential leadership in the state to the Democratic party. Politicians are nothing if not ambitious, and a future in the Republican party held few, if any, rewards in most areas of Virginia. The Democratic party, on the other hand, offered real opportunities for advancement—and victory at the polls if public office was the individual's goal. A person's beliefs or principles could be accommodated by the anti-Organization faction if not the Organization. The Democratic party offered possibility for advancement even to an individual opposed to the machine or, certainly, a better chance of advancement than would be afforded by membership in an antimachine Republican party. Thus, even a strong opposition to the ruling powers of the Democratic party would not encourage an individual to become active in the GOP.

The state Republicans did have one tool at their disposal which, if it had been· properly and wisely dispensed, could have partially overcome their multitudinous disadvantages and attracted more able leadership. That tool, of course, was patronage from the national Republican administrations. But, in fact, the powers in Virginia's GOP were encouraged to limit the party's growth because of patronage. The fewer leaders and officeholders, they reasoned, the more patronage they themselves would be able to control, dispense, and benefit from. A successful or even near successful contesting of statewide offices would draw more people to the party and inevitably result in a dilution of their authority and influence.

Development of Bifactionalism

This weakening of the Republican party by the development of a bifactional primary in Virginia was not a salutary development—at least not for anyone who believes in the basic efficacy of a two-party system. As reported earlier, Virginia's bifactional system was very much different from that of other southern states such as Florida, Texas, and Mississippi. "Virginia stands alone as a state in which one Democratic faction consistently commands the support of almost three-fourths of those who vote," concluded Key. There exists "almost a one-party system within a one-party system."[6] Although the lack of a runoff was in good part a

---

[6] Key, *Southern Politics*, p. 18. Georgia, North Carolina, Louisiana, and especially Tennessee all had some of the characteristics of a bifactional system, but none to the degree possessed by Virginia.

result of the bifactional nature of Virginia politics, its absence may actually have helped to reinforce bifactionalism. In southern states which early had instituted the runoff as part of the primary system, a fascinating summer election scenario developed. The first primary became the equivalent of a real primary nomination process in a regular two-party system, as a dozen or more candidates scrambled to gather enough votes to place first or second, thus to gain a berth in the second primary or runoff, which therefore became the equivalent of the general election. If a dual primary system encouraged multifactionalism, then it may also be reasonable to conclude that a uniprimary system encouraged bifactionalism. Even when Virginia did enact a statewide runoff statute in 1952 (the last southern state to do so), it was merely in response to one particular election aberration which had nearly cost the Organization the governorship. As such, the statute was seen more as an emergency escape clause for the machine than as a new and accepted part of the regular election machinery. Indeed, the runoff was not used for seventeen years after its adoption. Several of the differences in the Virginia runoff law compared to statutes in other southern states also suggest that the Old Dominion's second primary was not viewed as a regular necessity. The second-place finisher in Virginia, for example, had to file a request for the runoff, while other states provided for a mandatory runoff when a majority was not attained by one candidate in the first election.[7]

The factionalism which existed within the Democratic party was not a good substitute for two-party politics. Factions are fluid and discontinuous. They lack continuity in name and personnel and often, because of missing "party identification" voting cues, even in consistent support by groups of voters. Factions are confusing to voters, and without formal parties there is decidedly less issue content and follow-through once the candidates are in office because a reasonable system of accountability does not exist. The organization of factions is much looser than parties, and their structures are less firm and stable. There are no real patterns of

---

[7] In framing the statute in this fashion, the Byrd Organization may have been anticipating another situation like that in 1949, when a solid plurality voted for the Organization gubernatorial candidate, but a liberal challenger placed second. The other two candidates in the primary drew their votes from sectors of the Organization. Supposedly, then, the liberal challenger would see that with Organization voters unified in a runoff he would have little chance of victory, and consequently would decline to file for a runoff. Under the mandatory runoff system effective in other southern states, a second primary would have been automatically scheduled. The second-place finisher could still waive his right, of course, but this structural setup requires that a challenger take a positive action not to run, a less likely occurrence, perhaps, than forcing a positive action to run—and thereby causing the state to undertake an expensive and "unscheduled" election at public expense at the whim of a candidate.

breeding or developing leadership in some factions, notably (for Virginia at least) the out-of-power factions. All of the characteristics of factionalism just mentioned can be found in Virginia's Democratic party. For example, Key characterized the anti-Organization faction in the state as "extraordinarily weak, [with] few leaders of ability, and . . . more of a hope than a reality."[8] The Commonwealth's bifactionalism, however, prevented some of the more serious consequences of multifactionalism in a one-party system observed in other southern states. The above characteristics applied to Virginia were usually exaggerated by the chaos of multifactionalism, and other negative attributes developed as well. Demagogues flourished throughout the South, feeding on the individualistic politics encouraged by disorganized politics. Parties, on the other hand, usually worked to smooth out the "rough edges." Virginia's history and traditions made demagoguery an unwelcome and uncomfortable trade despite factionalism. The Virginia gentleman-voter usually rejected the crudities of the rabble-rouser and the overt Negro-baiter, and preferred a more genteel politics in concert with the Commonwealth's manner and tone.

A Historic Reversal

The rise of the primary as an institution in Virginia and the success which it enjoyed, then, are due to both the suffrage restrictions which established a stable and manageable electorate for the Organization and the complete subjugation of the Republican party accomplished by the 1902 Constitution and the primary itself. The decline of the primary can be understood from the vantage point of these same two factors—suffrage and Republican party. The legal changes occurring in the 1960s which were studied in the preceding chapter destroyed the restricted electorate and made continued Organization control of the primary exceedingly difficult. It is imperative to remember that an Organization is but a relatively small number of people, limited by its very nature and necessity, and it is humanly impossible for these individuals to control an electorate expanded beyond certain proportions, even when the composition of that electorate is relatively homogeneous. When the voting population becomes heterogeneous as well as expanded, the difficulties faced by a political Organization are exponentially increased. Even when Virginia had a homogeneous electorate prior to 1966, the Organization had considerable trouble in determining the electoral outcome. Both in 1928 and 1948 a presidential slate opposed by most or all of the Organization was comfortably endorsed

[8] Key, *Southern Politics*, p. 21.

by Virginians. In both of those years, too, the presidential election drew a much larger number of voters to the polls than in the succeeding gubernatorial primary and general elections, and it is reasonable to conclude that the Organization was not administratively or politically capable of controlling this swelled electorate. After 1966 the enrollment of large numbers of black and urban citizens created a permanent, heterogeneous voting population which would produce large turnouts in state elections as well as national. Clearly, the primary no longer had the stability provided by both Organization rule and a limited, homogeneous electorate. The primary elections went "out of control" and competition, costs, bitterness, and divisiveness increased as a result.

The Republican party was strengthened by the same forces which were weakening the Organization and its primary. The abolition of the poll tax and literacy tests helped to return the franchise to many Republicans throughout Virginia. Reapportionment would result in greater representation for the party in legislative halls. In turn, a greater measure of success for the GOP could attract more able leaders to the party's helm. A stronger party was capable of contesting elections in November. This "function"—providing two-party competition—helped to reverse the "institutional decay" within the party. The Republicans even won some general elections, first at the congressional district level and then for statewide office. The interest of the electorate began to shift from the primary, as turnout statistics in the next chapter will show, back to the general election. The primary was "tantamount time" no longer, as Republican victories pointed to the general election as the real point of final electoral decision. Many voters sat out the primary, which was now perceived as merely a "nominating" process, to wait and participate in the "final contest" in November.

A Changing Primary Electorate

This shift of interest from the primary to the general election had an interesting effect on the composition of the primary electorate in Virginia. That electorate became much blacker, more urban, and more liberal than the voting population as a whole.[9] While Virginia was a one-party state with a restricted suffrage, the primary vote was likely representative of the registered electorate overall. Key commented: "Perhaps in those one-party states with extremely high primary participation and in which the primary

[9] See data on Virginia urban and black voter participation from 1964 to 1973 in Sabato, *Aftermath of Armageddon.*

is indubitably the election the primary voters approximate a more or less representative sample of those who would vote in the general election if the general election were of any importance. Yet in states with a modicum of interparty competition primary participants are often by no means representative of the party."[10] Key's research indicated that the areas of a party's greatest strength tend to vote much more heavily in primaries in two-party competitive states.[11] Especially after 1966 this appeared to be the case in the Virginia Democratic primary. Urban, black, and liberal voters began to have a disproportionate influence in the primary. This meant, of course, that more liberal nominees were selected, and in conservative Virginia, especially as the ties of party loyalty were loosened, this meant added electoral opportunity for Republicans in November. Conservatives and some moderates became increasingly disenchanted with the Democratic party and would not support the candidates nominated in the primary. Many conservatives, for example, refused to support Democratic gubernatorial nominee William Battle in 1969 and cast their first Republican ballot on the statewide level for Linwood Holton, whom they perceived to be more conservative at that time. In 1970 many party moderates as well as conservatives refused to support liberal nominee George Rawlings, and instead voted for Independent Harry Byrd for the U.S. Senate. Thus, voting for a Republican or an Independent candidate was "legitimized" for thousands of formerly loyal moderate and conservative Democrats. Their voting patterns forced them to reconsider their party label, and many began to call themselves "Independent Democrats" or simply "Independents." The much-heralded party realignment of 1972 merely confirmed the exodus which had already taken place in the Democratic party. Conservatives and some moderates beforehand had lost interest in the liberal-dominated Democratic primary, and thus contributed to the development of an even more unrepresentative primary electorate. It was this limited voting population which could nominate the very liberal George Rawlings over a more moderate liberal, Clive DuVal, in the 1970 U.S. Senate primary. As Frank J. Sorauf correctly observed, a substantial sector of primary voters "generally comes from the party loyalists and activists. They are tuned to the cues of the party, but additionally they create problems for the party. They are often thought as a group to overrepresent issue and ideological concerns."[12]

[10] Key, *American State Politics*, p. 145.
[11] Key, *Southern Politics*, pp. 20–21.
[12] Sorauf, *Party Politics in America*, p. 218.

Other Factors in the Primary's Decline

Democrats of all factions also became disenchanted with the primary because of its practical impact on their candidates' fortunes. The growth of the Republican party meant that each party candidate faced a "double election." First, he had the hurdle of primary nomination, and then he was forced to do battle with his GOP opponent in the general election. The second election was the one that counted, but the first, less meaningful election drained many of the most valuable resources of candidate and party: money, time, organization, personal and party energies, and political stratagems. In 1969, for example, political reporters noted the obvious differences between the exhausted and worn Democrat, William C. Battle, a candidate in two hard-hitting primaries, and the relatively fresh and rested Republican, Linwood Holton, who had been nominated in a party convention. A confidential campaign memorandum prepared by Battle's managers in 1969 noted another dimension of the problem: "[Battle] faces the most difficult task of becoming a new face after months of continuous exposure." [13] The primary in Virginia, ever since the first in 1905, had "aired the dirty linen" of both candidates and party; yet there was little penalty to be paid in November since the moribund Republican party could hardly hope to capitalize on it successfully. The new reality of two-party competition, however, made the charges and counter-charges of a primary potentially very costly, providing the opposition with considerable ammunition gratis. The bitterness generated by a primary now could result directly or indirectly in Republican gain. First, voting for the Republican candidate now represented a viable and acceptable electoral decision, and a protest vote could be directly registered by an alienated Democrat. Or a bitter supporter of the primary loser could simply "go fishing" on election day, depriving the nominee of his much-needed support. A divisive primary in 1969 saw many thousands of liberal and conservative Democrats take one or another of these routes. [14]

[13] From "Prospectus on General Election," confidential memorandum, Battle for Governor campaign, Aug. 19, 1969. I came upon this memorandum in Henry Howell's files. There is no reason to doubt its authenticity (a disgruntled Battle worker turned it over to Howell during the campaign).

[14] Andrew Hacker presents statistics in his article, "Does a 'Divisive' Primary Harm a Candidate's Election Chances?" *American Political Science Review* 59 (1965): 105–10, to support his contention that the degree of primary competition has little effect on a candidate's performance in November. Although Hacker's data may be valid in the aggregate, there is little doubt that the 1969 primary in Virginia was a traumatic political experience for the Democratic party which left party unity in shambles and nominee William Battle vulnerable to Republican Holton. The general election returns by city and county, when compared to the primary and runoff results and past voting patterns of localities,

The result was the election of Republican Linwood Holton as governor. Clearly, the Democrats did not have the only party on the block; the GOP was present in November to pick up the pieces of a fratricidal primary battle. Even some party liberals began to question the wisdom of holding primary elections. Members of their faction could win the primaries, but what good were the nominations if their candidates were repeatedly rejected in November? The Rawlings victories of 1966 in the congressional primary and 1970 in the senatorial primary were frequently cited as empty triumphs. And the voter turnouts in primaries paid from the public treasury increasingly were becoming a source of embarrassment.

An institutional factor should be added to this explanation of the primary's decline. A court-ordered delay of the primaries in 1971, due to a redistricting dispute, caused much confusion in many legislative districts. The General Assembly had just completed a code revision which shifted the primary from July to June. In the midst of this change and consequent adjustments in local party and election machinery, the court delayed the primaries until September. [15] Faced with considerable uncertainty and disorientation, many localities turned to the convention method for the

---

clearly indicate that Howell supporters on the left and Pollard supporters on the right—some of whom did not participate in the primary elections—defected from the Democratic nominee in November. Comparative studies of predominantly black precincts and precincts which overwhelmingly supported George Wallace in the 1968 presidential election support this conclusion. Whether every divisive primary in Virginia would hurt the party candidate in November is unknown, but also irrelevant. The perception of damage has been firmly fixed in the minds of many Democratic party officials and voters and clearly affects their attitudes toward the primary.

[15] The date of the primary election in Virginia has changed numerous times throughout its history.

Before 1905—Each locality or legislative district set its own primary date. Thus no uniform primary date existed. No statewide primary was held.

1905-14—State party committee set date for statewide primaries (always sometime in August); local and district party committees set individual dates for all other primaries.

1915-52—Regulation by state statute hereafter. Local office primaries held on 1st Tuesday in April. State and district (includes congressional and state legislative elections) held on 1st Tuesday in August.

1953-70—Local: Unchanged. State and district: First primary held on the Tuesday after the 2d Monday in July. Runoff held on the 5th Tuesday after the first primary (mid-August).

1971—Court-ordered delay for district primaries until Sept. 14; no statewide primary held in this year; local primaries unaffected.

1972-present—Change in statutes passed in 1970 but implementation delayed by court in 1971. Local: 1st Tuesday in March. State and district: 2d Tuesday in June.

Source: *Acts of the Assembly 1900 [–1975]*.

first time in 1971. Once the procedures and guidelines for a convention were established, and a successful, smoothly run meeting was conducted (if this did indeed occur), a local party committee might be inclined, or at least less resistant, to employing the convention method of nomination in the future. Other institutional changes, such as the 1974 Gregg decision discussed earlier, helped to wean many cities and counties away from the primary.

Thus Democrats from all regions of Virginia began to confront some of the problems and frustrations voiced by Southwest Virginia at the 1904 state party convention. In earlier years Democrats delighted in deriding the "closed convention" of the Republicans, and pointed with pride to the contrast of their "open primary" method of nomination. As late as 1969 Democrats seemed to feel that this distinction had value to the voter. Some of William Battle's advisers, for example, suggested the campaign stress that "Battle is the 'People's Choice.' He was selected by the voters of Virginia. Holton was selected by a 'closed convention.' The Democrats of Virginia demonstrated during the primary campaigns that they were not the 'party of the past' or 'an old machine' but a young, vibrant force capable of discussing issues and offering new programs and solutions for Virginia's future."[16] The election results indicated that Virginia voters as a whole were little convinced by this argument, or perhaps cared less about the method of nomination than other considerations. The lesson of 1969 was not lost on the Democrats. Their party primary had played a major role in weakening the state GOP and in delaying the emergence of a full-fledged two-party system. But significant legal changes in the structure of the suffrage and representation in the middle 1960s had produced a historic reversal of party fortunes which culminated in the realignment of 1972 and the decline of the Democratic primary.

[16] "Prospectus on General Election."

Part IV

A Look to the Past and Future

Chapter 10

Seven Decades of the Primary:
A Statistical Summing-Up

JAMES THURBER once concluded one of his amusing fables with the moral: "There is no safety in numbers, or in anything else."[1] The data presented in this chapter are not intended to cloak the conclusions reached earlier in this study in the garb of infallibility—or incomprehensibility, as too often is the case when statistics are employed. Rather, the tables are used to compress and summarize the seven decades of the Virginia primary. It is hoped that the conclusions which have already been stated and the trends which have been identified will appear more distinct in this distilled form.

General Assembly Nomination

Although statewide primaries command most of the attention of public and press, the primary at the local level can provide a good deal more information for anyone interested in the development of nominating systems. Table 1 summarizes information on 1,768 Democratic nominations for the Virginia General Assembly between 1923 and 1975 (a year-by-year election breakdown can be found in Appendix V). Unfortunately newspaper reports—the only real source of data until a decade ago—were too incomplete to provide information before 1923, though legislative primaries were held in some localities like the cities of Richmond and Norfolk even before the founding of the statewide primary in 1905. Nevertheless, the fortunes of the primary system through the decades can be discerned in the more than a half century surveyed. The most striking feature as one scans the columns of table 1 vertically is the significant growth of the convention process and the tandem decrease in the number of contested seats in primaries as we approach 1975. In many years the largest number of nominations were won by candidates who were unopposed in the primaries. Even during the early years a hefty number of seats were uncontested. Never more than 66 percent of the nominations

---

[1] James Thurber, "The Fairly Intelligent Fly," *Fables for Our Times* (New York: Harper and Row, 1940), quoted in Edward R. Tufte, *Data Analysis for Politics and Policy* (Englewood Cliffs, N.J.: Prentice-Hall, 1974), p. xi.

Table 1. Methods of nomination for the Virginia General Assembly by the Democratic party, in selected years, 1923–75

| Years surveyed * | Method of nomination | | | | | | Total nominations |
| | Contested Primary | | Uncontested Primary | | Convention | | |
	No.	% of total	No.	% of total	No.	% of total	
1971–75	76	21.8	135	38.8	137	39.4	348
1963–67	154	37.6	196	47.8	60	14.6	410
1945–53	112	37.p	137	46.3	47	15.9	296
1933–37	168	50.2	123	36.7	44	13.1	335
1923–29	175	46.2	140	36.9	64	16.9	379
Total	685	38.7	731	41.4	352	19.9	1,768

Source: See Appendix V.
* Three General Assembly elections were surveyed in each of the sets of years listed. See Appendix V for exact election years.

for the House of Delegates or 53.6 percent of those for the state Senate were contested in the primaries. Except for the redistricting election of 1965, most later years show a considerable decrease in the number of nominees actually selected by primary.

There appear to have been fewer challenged seats when the threat to the Democratic party in the general election was greatest (or, at least, when such a threat was perceived at the time of the primary election). Two such cases are found in the years 1929 (which featured the anti-Smith upheaval and the "Coalitionist" opponents)[2] and 1973 (the age of party-switching, realignment, and great political uncertainty). The perception of the threat is most important. In November 1953 Republican Ted Dalton came close to upsetting the Democratic gubernatorial nominee, but this threat was not generally perceived at the time of filing for General Assembly primaries. Thus, the number of contests in the primaries is well within the normal range. Challenges were also noticeably fewer during the war years. After the major redistrictings of legislative seats in 1965 and 1971, there were more contests than usual. A large number of both new districts and legislative retirements (the latter partly a consequence of the former) help to explain this phenomenon. No attempt

[2] See note b in Appendix V for a full explanation.

can be made to interpret each fluctuation, since the number of primaries with and without opposing candidates held in a particular year depends upon so many variables (incumbency, local conditions, etc.) for which no data exist. Key has suggested that "the extent to which a party's nominations are contested in the primary by two or more aspirants depends in large measure on the prospects for victory for the nominee in the general election. Uncontested nominations for legislative posts are almost the rule in those districts in which a party's cause seems hopeless, while a large proportion of nominations are contested in relatively sure districts."[3] For the period before a strengthened Republican party could offer serious general election opposition, Key's suggestion would not appear to be valid for Virginia. The vast majority of seats that were not contested in primaries from 1923 to 1965 were held by incumbents. The advantages of incumbency would appear to explain the lack of primary opposition in many cases. "As for the power of the incumbent to discourage competition, it is one of the ironies of the primary. The primary really demands the kind of popular appeal and exposure which only the well-known incumbent often can muster. As a result, it creates the conditions that diminish its own effectiveness."[4] As we would expect, Republicans have nominated almost all of their General Assembly candidates by convention. Only in five years (1949, 1965, 1969, 1973, and 1975) has the GOP selected candidates by primary, and the number of primary nominees was small. It is easy to see why the Democratic primary was "tantamount to election," since in most years a majority of the Democratic nominees were not even opposed by Republicans in the general election.

Of the 1,768 nominations surveyed, a plurality of candidates (41.4 percent) were selected in unopposed elections. Primaries with opposing candidates accounted for 38.7 percent of the total, while conventions nominated only 19.9 percent over the entire period. Significant changes have occurred from decade to decade, however. The primaries in which opposing candidates ran accounted for only 21.8 percent of all nominations in the early 1970s. By contrast, 46.2 percent and 50.2 percent of legislative nominees were selected in such primaries in the 1920s and 1930s, respectively. One category—primaries with unopposed candidates—remained fairly constant throughout, ranging between 36.7 and 47.8 percent of each decade's nomination total. The number of convention nominations has skyrocketed of late. For the first time conventions selected a plurality (39.4 percent) of Democratic General Assembly

[3] Key, *American State Politics*, p. 172.
[4] Sorauf, *Party Politics in America*, p. 217.

nominees in the 1970s. In previous decades the convention percentages had ranged only between 13.1 and 16.9. The reasons for this sudden change at the end of the 1960s have already been discussed, of course, and the figures in table 1 help to confirm the alteration in Democratic nomination modes after the 1969 gubernatorial election, in particular.

Some comparative statistics exist for other states on the degree of competition in legislative primaries. While Virginia's average of no opposition against 41.4 percent of its primary candidates may appear high, other states have even less competition and more uncontested elections. In a Pennsylvania study 58.6 percent of all Democrats and 62.8 percent of all Republicans were unopposed in primaries for the state legislature. In Wisconsin, the home of the modern primary system, the number of contested primary seats is only about 10 percent higher than in Pennsylvania.[5]

Regional Patterns

A regional study of Virginia's legislative primaries can also prove instructive (see table 2; Appendix VI contains a more detailed breakdown of regional data). The Commonwealth's regions were outlined in figure 1, and it should be noted that they do not contain equal population or an equivalent number of legislators. The Tidewater region (with the six Hampton Roads cities deleted) has never had but a few legislators, while the Northern Virginia region, especially after recent redistrictings, has had many state representatives. These considerations must be borne in mind when making regional comparisons.

It is immediately apparent that the Southwest and Shenandoah regions, as we would expect, have had few primaries, and in more than half of the years surveyed, not a single primary election was held in either area. The West, Tidewater (minus Hampton Roads), and especially the Southside formerly had a larger number of primaries than at present. The Northern Neck—Eastern Shore and Piedmont regions also have recorded a considerable reduction in the number of primaries held. In absolute numbers the Hampton Roads, Richmond, and Northern Virginia areas have held steady.

Most of the explanation for the reduction of regional primaries is found in the growth of the convention system. Redistricting has also

[5] Sorauf, *Party and Representation: Legislative Politics in Pennsylvania* (New York: Atherton Press, 1963), p. 111. The Pennsylvania average for candidates of both parties was 60.7 percent unopposed.

Table 2. Democratic primary elections for the Virginia General Assembly, by regions and by decades

Region	No. of primary elections held in region (% of total for decade)						
	1920–29*	1930–39	1940–49	1950–59	1960–69	1970–75	Total
Northern							
Virginia	6 (5.4)	11 (5.0)	16 (12.2)	16 (12.9)	13 (13.1)	11 (33.3)	73 (10.2)
Piedmont	23 (20.7)	45 (20.5)	3 (22.9)	22 (17.7)	13 (13.1)	2 (6.1)	135 (18.8)
Northern Neck-							
Eastern							
Shore	15 (13.5)	26 (11.9)	12 (9.2)	13 (10.5)	7 (7.1)	3 (9.1)	76 (10.6)
Richmond	10 (9.0)	15 (6.8)	7 (5.3)	11 (8.9)	13 (13.1)	5 (15.2)	61 (8.5)
Hampton							
Roads	16 (14.4)	35 (16.0)	19 (14.5)	26 (21.0)	22 (22.2)	7 (21.2)	125 (17.4)
Tidewater							
excluding							
H.R.	9 (8.1)	11 (5.0)	2 (1.5)	2 (1.6)	1 (1.0)	0 (0.0)	25 (3.5)
Southside	19 (17.1)	47 (21.5)	30 (22.9)	20 (16.1)	16 (16.2)	5 (15.2)	137 (19.1)
Southwest	2 (1.8)	6 (2.7)	0 (0.0)	1 (0.8)	4 (4.0)	0 (0.0)	13 (1.8)
West	10 (9.0)	19 (8.7)	12 (9.2)	12 (9.7)	9 (9.1)	0 (0.0)	62 (8.6)
Shenandoah							
Valley	1 (0.9)	4 (1.8)	3 (2.3)	1 (0.8)	1 (1.0)	0 (0.0)	10 (1.4)
Total for							
decade	111	219	131	124	99	33	717

Source: See Appendix VI.
Note: See figure 1 for exact description of Virginia's regional areas. See Appendix VI for definitions of terms used in this table and for other explanatory footnotes.
* The elections surveyed in this decade are those held in 1923, 1927, and 1929.

played a significant role, particularly in the Southside and Northern Neck–Eastern Shore where the number of legislators has been considerably reduced by recent reapportionments. In the 1970s primaries became predominantly an urban phenomenon. Whereas in 1923 only 26.5 percent of all primaries were held in urban areas, in 1971 metropolitan localities accounted for 61 percent of primary nominations, and in 1975 eleven of thirteen primaries (85 percent) were held in urban Virginia.[6]

The state's capital could also be termed the capital of the Virginia primary. In only two of twenty-six years did Richmond fail to hold a legislative primary election. Further, it was not unusual to have twenty

[6] This trend is relatively recent as well. In 1961 only 44 percent of all primaries were held in urban areas, and in 1963 the figure was 42 percent. Still, considerable increase from the earlier years of the primary is indicated.

or more candidates contesting the city's five to seven House of Delegates seats. Norfolk was also the site of frequent primaries, but on the average the number of candidates was many fewer than Richmond's annual crop. With the exception of 1949 when Norfolk and Bedford had GOP primaries, the Republican party primaries have been exclusively a Northern Virginia phenomenon. This is not surprising, since the Eighth Congressional District was the birthplace of the GOP primary in Virginia, and Northern Virginia Republicans have found in their ranks over the last quarter century many advocates of the primary system.

Table 2 indicates regional trends more clearly in a summary of the data by decades. Northern Virginia in the 1920s accounted for only 5.4 percent of primary nominations, but in the 1970s a full third of the primary elections were being held there. Further, the cities and counties of the Washington, D.C., suburbs were the only localities which showed an absolute increase in the number of primaries from 1920 to 1970. Numerically, the number of primaries has decreased in every other region— further testimony to the increasing strength of the convention nominating method. Richmond and Hampton Roads did register an increase in the proportion of the statewide total of primaries being held in those regions. Elsewhere, the decline of primaries is dramatic. Only the Southwest and the Shenandoah Valley show stability, since there were virtually no primary nominations throughout the entire period.

The pattern of primaries in the 1950s compared to that in the 1970s gives an indication of the numerical and regional trends in primary and convention nominations. In the earlier time period, primaries were held in cities and counties all over the state, except for the Southwest and the Valley. There was as much primary activity in the western part of the state as the eastern. But the differences are sharp in the 1970s. All but three of the fifteen cities holding primaries were in the urban corridor; all but one of these primary cities also held primaries in the 1950s. The same changes can be seen in Virginia's counties, and the primary predominates only in the eastern, urban corridor area. The influence of the convention was growing as the primary declined. The same conclusion is reached by examining the convention pattern for one year close to the primary's origin and one year near the start of its decline. In 1913 only thirteen counties and four cities held a convention. The great bulk of these localities were found in the Southwest and in far western Southside. In the rest of the state only one Shenandoah Valley county, one Piedmont county and one county of the West dared to defy the mighty primary. But in 1975 one might suggest that the primary had become "unconventional." The convention system had a stronger base in the western half of Virginia and had extended its influence east. All of the Southwest, all of the West, all of the Valley, all far west and a few central Southside localities, and most of the western Piedmont had come under the domain of the nominating convention. Even Harry Byrd, Sr.'s home base in Winchester had fallen away from the primary. Still, only a few urban corridor localities had succumbed to the trend, and Petersburg was the farthest eastern advance of the convention. Almost all areas now using the convention system have adopted it since 1967. The only localities consistently using the convention are found in the Southwest. Thirty-three cities and counties are located between these extremes. Some Shenandoah, western Southside, West, and a few Southwest localities have historically alternated between use of the primary and convention. Overall, the number of localities holding conventions remained fairly constant until 1967, when a rapid growth in the system's popularity began.[7]

Nominations for the U.S. House of Representatives

A look at congressional primaries is also in order, and table 3 presents Democratic primary data at the district level from 1952 to 1974. In any one of the twelve election years surveyed, there were never more than three contested primaries in the ten congressional districts. Overall, only 18.2 percent of the congressional nominations have been contested in the primaries. This is a considerably smaller proportion than the percentage of General Assembly contested primary nominations since 1952 (32.0 percent). Almost half of the nominations for the U.S. House of Representatives were unopposed, and the rest of the nominees (about one-third) were selected by convention. Incumbency is certainly a factor in the lack of opposition in congressional primaries; turnover of congressmen is low relative to that of state legislators. Also, congressional primaries (for U.S. Senate and House) occur in presidential election years, while all Assembly and state office nominations are scheduled for off years. A presidential election holds the possibility of coattail benefits for the GOP, and this threat to Democratic party hegemony may have discouraged primary competition. (Earlier it was suggested that competition for General Assembly seats in the primary declined in years where there were perceptible threats in November.) Some evidence can be found from the data in table 3 to support this suggestion, since only six of twenty primaries

---

[7] The number of localities holding a convention was determined from newspaper accounts for eleven years: 1913 (20 conventions); 1929 (25); 1933 (18); 1935 (21); 1937 (14); 1945 (18); 1949 (15); 1953 (18); 1967 (41); 1973 (57); 1975 (75).

Table 3. Democratic primary elections for U.S. House of Representatives in Virginia, 1952-74

Year	No. of contested primaries	No. of uncontested primaries	No. of conventions
1954	2	5	3
1956	1	6	3
1958	2	5	3
1960	0	N.A.	N.A.
1962	2	5	3
1964	1	6	3
1966	3	5	2
1968	1	6	3
1970	3	5	2
1972 *	1	5	4
1974	2	3	5
Total	20 (18.2%)	53 (48.2%)	37 (33.6%)

Source: Compiled from figures supplied by the State Board of Elections.
Note: Virginia had ten congressional districts throughout the years surveyed. See Appendix I for a description of those districts.
N.A.: Not available.
* The Republican party in Virginia held a congressional primary in the Eighth Congressional District in 1972. Republican congressional primaries were also held in the Eighth District in 1948 and 1950. These three primaries are the only congressional primaries ever held by the Republican party.

with opposition were held in presidential years. The small number of congressional primaries surveyed makes any conclusions tenuous, however. There was some growth in the use of the convention in the last two elections,[8] and there was certainly no growth in the number of primaries, nor is any such growth in prospect. Yet again, no firm conclusions should be drawn. One statement can be made with certainty: the preference of Republicans for conventions is indicated once again

[8] The year 1952 shows an exceptionally large number of conventions. It appears that this phenomenon was related to both the nominating convenience of district conclaves already scheduled to prepare for the 1952 state and national Democratic conventions and the very real threat of a Republican landslide in November. The latter was definitely perceived at primary time and could well have encouraged district party officials (as well as the incumbent congressmen) to nominate by the most efficient, unifying, and least troublesome method. The Republicans did elect three of their nominees to the U.S. House in November, thanks to the overwhelming Virginia victory of Dwight Eisenhower; thus, Democratic fears were justified. In any event, the phenomenon has not been repeated, although as the text notes there have been fewer contested congressional primaries in presidential election years.

in the congressional arena. Only three GOP congressional district primaries—all in the Northern Virginia Eighth—have been recorded in this century.

The regional pattern of congressional primaries confirms the observations made from the study of General Assembly contests (see table 4). The large number of primaries without opposition in the First, Second, Third, Fourth, and Fifth congressional districts was due to well-entrenched incumbents. Normally, we would expect to see contests in at least the Norfolk-area Second and Richmond-area Third. The congressional primary has proved most popular in the Northern Virginia Tenth, which recorded seven opposed elections out of eleven surveyed. The conventions were most popular in the Ninth district, of course. As best as could be determined, the Ninth has never held a congressional primary. Conventions also proved popular in the Republican-infested Sixth and Seventh districts. The Eighth District is a special case which should be noted. Heavily redistricted in the last two decades, the Eighth has been transformed from a predominantly rural to a wholly urban-suburban district. During its rural days party leaders in the Eighth favored conventions, while since 1966 primaries have been the rule as new leadership has emerged in the district. The composition of the Fourth District has also been radically changed, but conventions rather than primaries have been favored by the new party leaders.[9]

Participation in Primaries

Voter turnout in primary elections has been extremely low throughout the history of the primary in Virginia—even after the expansion of the electorate in the 1960s. During the years of Organization rule, the poll tax, literacy tests, and other registration hardships were the main reasons for the poor voting participation. Moger added one further and important explanation: "Apathy resulting from the one-party system was and continued to be the greatest cause [of low turnout]. . . . A general consciousness that the machine produced above-average government also encouraged the habit."[10] After the suffrage restrictions were finally removed in the middle 1960s, the voter's focus shifted away from the primary and toward the general election, so that the primary participation rate remained low. The voting age population turnouts and

---

[9] For more detail on the Eighth and Fourth districts, see note to table 4 and also the congressional district maps in Appendix I.

[10] Moger, p. 354.

Table 4. Nominating methods of the Democratic party for U.S. House of Representatives, by districts, 1952–74

Congressional district*	No. of contested primaries	No. of uncontested primaries	No. of conventions
1	1	9	1
2	2	8	1
3	1	10	0
4	1	7	3
5	0	10	1
6	3	1	7
7	1	4	6
8	5	0	6
9	0	0	11
10	7	4	0

Source: Compiled from figures supplied by the State Board of Elections.
Note: See Appendix I which shows Virginia's congressional districts from 1952 to the present. Virginia had ten congressional districts throughout the years surveyed. Figures for the number of unopposed primaries and the number of conventions held were not available for 1960.
* The boundaries of the ten congressional districts were changed by redistrictings in the 1960s and 1970s. Most districts, however, retained the bulk of their territory after the redistrictings, so that the city and county composition of the district Democratic committees was fairly stable. (These committees usually determine the method by which the party nominees are chosen.) Two exceptions should be noted, however. The boundaries of the Fourth and Eighth districts have changed radically since 1952. These formerly large rural enclaves became smaller and urban dominated.

percentages garnered by the winners in all statewide primaries in Virginia are compiled in table 5. There is some variation in the participation rates within a narrow range, and this fluctuation is primarily due to the degree of competition in each primary. In 1948, for example, a sluggish Senate contest in which A. Willis Robertson was the overwhelming favorite resulted in a low 7.2 percent turnout. But in 1952 Francis Miller ran a brisk and lively campaign against Byrd, more than doubling the turnout from 1948. The 1949 Battle versus Miller gubernatorial primary produced the record turnout for all years, with the total vote perhaps abnormally inflated with a larger-than-usual Republican contingent. In 1957 there was little primary competition for governor, but four years later a hotly contested race developed, and this was reflected in the relative turnouts.

Table 5. Voting participation in Democratic primary elections in Virginia, 1905–70

Year	Total primary vote	Percentage of voting age population*	
		Total vote	Vote for winner
1905 U.S. Senate	82,998	18.5	10.4
1905 Governor	83,206	18.5	9.5
1909 Governor	73,484	16.4	8.7
1911 U.S. Senate	96,646	18.5	12.5
1911 U.S. Senate (special)	96,254	18.4	12.9
1913 Governor†	68,730	13.1	9.1
1917 Governor	89,565	17.1	7.5
1921 Governor	150,699	12.5	7.2
1922 U.S. Senate	139,716	11.6	8.5
1925 Governor	174,896	14.5	8.9
1929 Governor	138,253	11.5	8.6
1933 Governor	189,623	14.5	9.0
1937 Governor	193,274	14.8	12.8
1941 Governor	137,974	8.7	6.7
1945 Governor	138,788	8.8	6.2
1946 U.S. Senate	223,528	14.2	9.0
1948 U.S. Senate	114,268	7.2	5.1
1949 Governor	316,622	20.1	8.6
1952 U.S. Senate	345,307	17.0	10.7
1953 Governor	228,214	11.2	7.4
1957 Governor	150,101	7.4	5.9
1961 Governor	352,158	15.2	8.6
1966 U.S. Senate	433,159	18.7	9.4
1966 U.S. Senate (special)	434,217	18.7	9.5
1969 Governor	408,630	17.6	6.9
1969 Governor (run-off)	433,613	18.7	9.8
1970 U.S. Senate	128,959	4.6	2.1

Sources: Voting age population figures were computed from table 21, p. 55, of U.S. Bureau of the Census, *Census of Population 1970, General Population Characteristics: Final Report PC(1)-B48 Virginia.* Primary vote totals were taken from Appendixes III and IV (see these appendixes for further explanation of sources).

* From 1905 to 1919 voting age population is the total male population age 21 and over. Voting age population for all years after 1919 is the total population age 21 and over. The following decennial voting age population figures were used in this table: 1900, 449,206; 1910, 523,262; 1920, 1,206,082; 1930, 1,303,934; 1940, 1,578,224; 1950, 2,028,529; 1960, 2,316,924; and 1970, 2,796,325.

† There was only one candidate for governor, but there were contests for lieutenant governor and attorney general. Voter turnout shown is the vote cast for lieutenant governor—the higher vote of the two offices.

One major suffrage change—the extension of the franchise to women in 1920—actually resulted in a decrease in the overall participation rate. Despite an increase in the absolute vote cast, women apparently did not participate at the same rate as men, resulting in a drop in the average percentage of turnout.[11] Many women were undoubtedly discouraged from voting by their husbands, and ridicule combined with unfamiliarity with the voting process itself took a toll. The participation of women was hardly welcomed by public officeholders, especially those in the Organization. "Some believed it was against the dignity of women to enter the political hustlings, . . . but the real fear in Virginia and the South was that in enforcing the Nineteenth Amendment the federal government would also enforce the Fifteenth, 'thus overthrowing white supremacy, pure elections, and the Democratic party.' "[12] In 1919 the House of Delegates rejected the Nineteenth Amendment by 61 to 21, and the state Senate refused ratification by 19 to 15. Indeed, almost a half century passed before the General Assembly "ratified" the Women's Rights Amendment—long after its effective date.

Before 1920 about 16 to 18 percent of the potentially eligible voters actually participated in the primary. After women received the vote and thereby increased the pool of potential voters, turnout fell to 11-14 percent. The years of the Second World War brought participation to an even lower level of under 9 percent. Only in the postwar years did the participation rate occasionally reach the pre–Nineteenth Amendment turnout levels, but even in this era participation averaged only 13.2 percent. The end of the poll tax and literacy tests and the passage of the Voting Rights Act in 1965 greatly increased the absolute vote cast, but the simultaneous enlargement of the registered vote meant only a small recorded increase in turnout percentages through 1969. The disastrous turnout in the 1970 primary confirmed the loss of interest in the primary among the state's voting population. Only 4.6 percent of the potential voters cast a ballot, in the lowest statewide primary turnout ever. As one commentator suggested, the state's voters had answered the question: "What if they gave a primary and nobody came?" Yet the 1970 election was only the culmination of a trend begun in 1966. In fact, five primaries held before the legal changes in the suffrage had higher turnouts than any of the primary elections held after the changes.

The percentage of the potential electorate which nominated Virginia's Democratic candidates was incredibly small. At best the officeseeker

[11] A similar effect was noted nationally after the extension of the franchise to 18-20-year-olds in 1971.

[12] Moger, p. 328; see also Gooch, pp. 5-6.

had the endorsement of 12.9 percent (Claude Swanson in the 1911 Senate race) and 12.8 percent (James H. Price in the 1937 governor's contest) of the potential electorate. At worst, the winner of a primary could count in his corner only 5.1 percent (Senator Robertson in 1948) or 5.9 percent (J. Lindsay Almond for governor in 1957) of the voting age population. In 1970 a pitiful 2.1 percent of the potential electorate nominated George Rawlings for the U.S. Senate.

Participation in Virginia and the Nation

How does Virginia compare with the rest of the nation in competition and participation in primary elections? The findings of studies on other states show that there are fewer primary contestants in elections where incumbents are seeking renomination.[13] Virginia certainly fits this pattern, especially with regard to U.S. Senate primaries. Only ten of twenty-seven Senate races in primaries since 1905 (37 percent) have been contested. Of those ten, four challenges were to previously unelected or appointed incumbents. One primary with opposing candidates (1970) had no incumbent. Further, in only six of seventeen cases (35.3 percent) in which the incumbent lieutenant governor or attorney general sought renomination was there opposition in the primary. Research by V. O. Key, Jr., on primaries from 1920 to 1954 indicated that only 10 percent of incumbent U.S. senators seeking renomination were defeated.[14] Yet 30 percent of all southern U.S. senators seeking renomination were defeated, compared to 2 percent in nonsouthern states, since the only chance to defeat a Dixie senator came in the primary. Virginia's record is much different from the one which Key's study would have suggested. Only one Virginia U.S. Senate incumbent, A. Willis Robertson in 1966, was ever defeated for renomination. As such, Virginia is much closer to the nonsouthern average than to the record of its sister states of the South. In addition, only one of seventeen incumbent lieutenant governors or attorneys general who sought renomination was ever defeated in Virginia, Attorney General Samuel W. Williams in 1913. These figures are further evidence of both the stability provided by the Old Dominion's bifactional system and the degree of success experienced by and control exerted by the Organization.

Another conclusion reached by many researchers of primary trends in other states is that the better a party's chances of winning the

[13] Austin Ranney, "Parties in State Politics," in Jacob and Vines, pp. 96–99.
[14] Key, *Politics, Parties, and Pressure Groups*, p. 441.

general election, then the greater the chance for contests in primaries, especially if the incumbent is not seeking reelection.[15] At the statewide level Virginia also conforms to this axiom's electoral implications. In the gubernatorial races (where the incumbent is constitutionally barred from seeking reelection) fourteen of fifteen primaries saw contests during the period of absolute Democratic dominance of the general election, 1905–61. Only in 1913 was the candidate for governor unopposed. In twelve of fifteen primaries where there was no incumbent lieutenant governor or attorney general seeking renomination, the posts were contested. But after the GOP became a general election threat on the statewide level, in only three of nine primaries were the candidates for governor, lieutenant governor, and attorney general opposed.

Finally, national studies have suggested that, except for the states of the one-party South, voting turnout is markedly lower in primaries than in general elections.[16] As table 6 proves, this conclusion is also valid for Virginia. The one-party system which existed before 1965 in the Commonwealth produced turnouts in five gubernatorial primaries (1925, 1933, 1937, 1941, and 1949) which actually exceeded the general election vote by 11 to 23 percent. Another governor's primary (1917) had a turnout which was virtually identical to that of the general election. Only rarely did the general election produce a vote greatly exceeding the primary total, and in those cases, a minimally contested primary, such as that of 1957, was usually to blame. Also, presidential elections greatly swelled the general election vote beyond normal proportions in 1948 and 1952. Twice, however, vigorous Republican competition in November (in the years 1929 and 1953) heightened interest in the general election and produced a vote almost double that of the primary election. However, these were clearly exceptions to the rule during Virginia's one-party days. As Virginia became more two-party competitive in the 1960s, this relationship between primary and general election turnout also began to shift, and the Commonwealth approached the experience of other states which possessed two strong parties. Despite fiercely contested primaries in 1966 and 1969, the total general election vote far exceeded the primary total, and in 1970 the general election recorded a turnout more than seven times greater than the primary. Additional data on primary and general election turnouts appear in tables 7 and 8, which indicate the relative interest shown by voters from one election to the next. In the gubernatorial primaries, the excitement generated by the first primary in 1905 resulted in a large vote not matched again until 1917. After the increase brought

[15] Ranney in Jacob and Vines, pp. 96–99.
[16] Ibid; see also Key, *Politics, Parties, and Pressure Groups*, p. 379 (Table 14.1).

Table 6. Voting participation in general elections in Virginia, 1905–70

Year		Total general election vote	Percentage of voting age population	Percentage of primary vote
1905	Governor	130,561	29.1	157.3
1909	Governor	118,666	26.4	142.6
1917	Governor	89,812	17.2	100.3
1921	Governor	210,863	17.5	139.9
1922	U.S. Senate	161,923	13.4	115.9
1925	Governor	144,973	12.0	82.9
1929	Governor	269,728	22.4	195.1
1933	Governor	166,568	12.8	87.8
1937	Governor	149,972	11.5	77.6
1941	Governor	122,463	7.8	88.8
1945	Governor	168,783	10.7	121.6
1946	U.S. Senate	252,863	16.0	113.1
1948	U.S. Senate	386,998	24.5	338.7
1949	Governor	262,350	16.6	82.9
1952	U.S. Senate	543,516	26.8	157.4
1953	Governor	414,025	20.4	181.4
1957	Governor	517,655	25.5	344.9
1961	Governor	394,490	17.0	112.0
1966	U.S. Senate	733,879	31.7	169.4
1966	U.S. Senate (special)	729,839	31.5	168.1
1969	Governor	915,764	39.5	224.1
1969	Governor (run-off)	915,764	39.5	211.2
1970	U.S. Senate	946,751	33.9	734.1

Sources: Voting age population figures were computed from table 21, p. 55, of U.S. Bureau of the Census, *Census of Population 1970, General Population Characteristics: Final Report PC(1)-B48 Virginia.* A combination of four sources was used to determine the total general election vote for the years listed in this table: canvass results published in state newspapers, the *Annual Reports of the Secretary of the Commonwealth to the Governor and General Assembly*, official election results provided by the State Board of Elections, and Edward Franklin Cox, *State and National Voting in Federal Elections, 1910–1970* (Hamden, Conn.: Shoe String Press), 1972.

Note: The voting age population is defined in the notes to table 5. General elections for an office are listed in this table only if a Democratic primary election for the same office was held in the same year. Democratic primaries were held for the U.S. Senate in 1905 and 1911, but there were no general elections for the seat since final selection still rested with the General Assembly.

Table 7. Changes in voting participation in Virginia gubernatorial elections, 1905–69

Year	Primary election vote total	Percentage increase or decrease from preceding primary	General election vote total	Percentage increase or decrease from preceding general election
1905	83,206	—	130,561	—
1909	73,484	-11.7	118,666	-9.1
1917	89,565	+21.9	89,812	-24.3
1921	150,699	+68.3	210,863	+134.8
1925	174,896	+16.1	144,973	-31.2
1929	138,253	-21.0	269,728	+86.1
1933	189,623	+37.2	166,568	-38.2
1937	193,274	+1.9	149,972	-10.0
1941	137,974	-28.6	122,463	-18.3
1945	138,788	+0.6	168,783	+37.8
1949	316,622	+128.1	262,350	+55.4
1953	228,214	-27.9	414,025	+57.8
1957	150,101	-34.2	517,655	+25.0
1961	352,158	+134.6	394,490	-23.8
1969	408,630	+16.0	915,764	+132.1
1969*	433,613	+23.1	915,764	+132.1

Sources: See tables 5 and 6.
* Runoff election for governor. The preceding primary election is the 1961 primary, and the preceding general election is also 1961.

Table 8. Changes in voting participation in Virginia U.S. Senate elections, 1905–70

Year	Primary election vote total	Percentage increase or decrease from preceding primary	General election vote total*	Percentage increase or decrease from preceding general election
1905	82,998	—	—	—
1911†	96,646	+16.4	—	—
1922	139,716	+44.6	161,923	—
1946	223,528	+60.0	252,863	+56.2
1948‡	114,268	-48.9	386,998	+53.1
1952‡	345,307	+202.2	543,516	+40.4
1966‡	433,159	+25.4	733,879	+35.0
1970	128,959	-70.2	946,751	+29.0

Sources: see tables 5 and 6.
* The General Assembly elected U.S. senators until 1913. Thus there were no general elections for U.S. Senate in 1905 and 1911.
† Election results for the regular election for a six-year term are used in this table for those years in which two simultaneous U.S. Senate elections were held.
‡ Denotes presidential election year.

by the enfranchisement of women, the turnout trend was remarkably constant in the primaries, with a large increase recorded after World War II and in 1961 (following two listless primary contests). The increases in the 1969 primaries were not as great as one might have expected, but a major increase over 1961 is reflected in the 1969 general election vote. The turnout progression in senatorial contests shows steady increases in the general election vote with considerable variation in the relative primary votes, for reasons which have already been discussed.

From One-Party to Two-Party System

Some proof that Virginia is moving from a modified one-party system to a full-fledged two-party system can be found in table 9. The percen-

Table 9. Mean voting turnout in primary and general elections for governor and U.S. senator, 1962–68, for all states

State groups (number of states)*	Percentage voting for governor†			Percentage voting for U.S. senator†		
	Primary election	General election	Dif-ference	Primary election	General election	Dif-ference
One-party Democratic (7)	35.9	36.2	-0.3	28.1	33.4	-5.3
Modified one-party Democratic (10)	33.5	49.9	-16.4	23.9	46.7	-22.8
Two-party (28)	28.1	60.7	-32.6	26.4	61.3	-34.9
Modified one-party Republican (5)	24.4	64.6	-40.2	19.5	58.6	-39.1
Virginia (1946–61)‡	13.5	19.9	-6.4	12.8	22.4	-9.6
Virginia (1962–70)§	18.2	39.5	-21.3	14.0	32.4	-18.4

Sources: Adapted from Austin Ranney, "Parties in State Politics," in Herbert Jacobs and Kenneth N. Vines, eds., *Politics in the American States* (Boston: Little, Brown, and Co., 1971), p. 98, table 3. Virginia statistics compiled from official election results provided by the State Board of Elections.

* For list of states in each grouping, see Jacobs and Vines, p. 87. Virginia is considered a "modified one-party Democratic state."

† Percentages refer to the potential vote (total population age 21 and older).

‡ Mean for all primary elections held in Virginia from 1946 to 1961. Four gubernatorial and three Senate primaries were held during those years.

§ Mean for all primary elections held in Virginia from 1962 to 1970. Two gubernatorial and three Senate primaries were held during those years.

tage of the electorate voting for governor and U.S. senator in the primary versus the general election is compared for various groupings of states. The primary in Virginia is clearly becoming less important. For Virginia gubernatorial races from 1946 to 1961, there was only a 6.4 percent difference in turnout between primary and general election—a result which places Virginia closest to the one-party Democratic states. For the period 1962–70, however, the turnout difference between primary and general elections (21.3 percent) positions Virginia much closer to the two-party states. In Senate elections from 1946 to 1961, there was only a 9.6 percent difference in turnout, even with two of three Senate elections occurring in a presidential year. The Senate percentage difference had almost doubled to 18.4 during the later period, however, and this difference is understated since all three elections occurred in nonpresidential years. Modern Virginia would have been positioned much closer to the two-party states in the Senate category had only nonpresidential election years been used throughout the table.

Virginia's unique bifactionalism is also confirmed in table 10, where

Table 10. Average number of Democratic candidates for governor in southern states, 1919–75

State	Governor	
	Number of primary contests*	Average number of candidates per primary†
Florida	16	4.6
Mississippi	15	4.3
Louisiana	15	4.2
Alabama	14	3.8
South Carolina	13	3.1
Arkansas	28	3.5
Texas	27	3.5
Georgia	20	3.1
North Carolina	13	3.1
Tennessee	23	2.6
Virginia	12	2.4

Source: Compiled from Congressional Quarterly, Inc., *Guide to U.S. Elections* (Washington, D.C.: Congressional Quarterly, 1975), pp. 897–908. For Virginia, source data are found in Appendix II. The State Board of Elections and the Office of the Secretary of State provided the 1975 election returns for Mississippi and Louisiana.
* Only contested primaries were included in this table. In states with runoff primaries, only the first primaries were counted.
† Only candidates who received at least 5 percent of the vote are counted.

data are compiled on the average number of Democratic primary candidates in the South from 1919 to 1975. The Old Dominion has the lowest average number of candidates for governor (2.4) in all of Dixie. Tennessee and North Carolina also have relatively small fields of primary candidates, but this is in good measure accounted for by the strength of their state Republican parties rather than a strict and formalized bifactional structure which Virginia alone possessed. The startling situation of multifactionalism can be seen in this table as well. Florida averaged 4.6 gubernatorial candidates, and Mississippi and Louisiana were not far behind. Note that only candidates who received at least 5 percent of the vote were counted in table 10. If all candidates who qualified for the gubernatorial primaries were included, the disparity between Virginia and the other southern states would be much greater still.

Much has already been written about the effect which urbanization and the enrollment of black voters had upon the Organization and, ultimately, the Democratic primary. It is interesting to note that even with a select and restricted electorate, Organization candidates always fared more poorly in the urban corridor than outside of it, as table 11 indicates. The growth of that corridor signified increasing trouble for the machine, as urban and suburban localities accounted for an even larger percentage of the total vote. The rural-based Organization had always accommodated the views of its Southside brethren, to the detriment of the urban citizenry, and this was not forgotten at the polling booth. Neither did black voters forget that the machine had drawn its strongest support from white supremacists in cities and counties with large black populations.[17] In his 1952 primary race for reelection to the U.S. Senate, for example, Harry Byrd, Sr., carried all but four localities with black populations exceeding 30 percent. The one county in this category which Byrd failed to carry was Charles City County, which had a black population at the time of 81 percent. The three largely black-populated cities which Byrd lost were all located in Tidewater (Hampton, Newport News, and Portsmouth), a region which was traditionally anti-Byrd for the traditional reasons.

In this chapter the Democratic primary has been turned statistically upside down and inside out in an attempt to clarify and summarize the trends observed in the course of its history. But there are still further questions which should be answered. What is the future of the Democratic

[17] This is not surprising, of course, since whites residing in areas where blacks were numerous and visible would naturally be most conscious of the racial issue—a question on which the Organization always made its stand very clear. Interestingly, George Wallace's 1968 presidential bid was most successful in those same black-populated cities and counties, probably for the same reason. See Sabato, *Aftermath of Armageddon*, which contains a detailed analysis of the Wallace vote in Virginia.

primary in Virginia? More precisely, what should be the future of the primary? What are the alternatives? The concluding section will attempt to address these important issues.

Table 11. Democratic primary vote in the urban corridor, 1945–69

			Vote in urban corridor		
Year	Office	Organization candidate	Percentage of total vote	Percentage for Organization candidate	Percentage for Organization candidate outside corridor
1945	Governor	Tuck	42.8	62.0	76.2
1946	Senator	Byrd, Sr.	42.5	54.1	70.4
1949	Governor	Battle*	44.0	36.7	47.6
1952	Senator	Byrd, Sr.	45.2	58.2	66.4
1961	Governor	Harrison	52.9	52.7	61.1
1966	Senator	Byrd, Jr.	59.8	44.9	59.0
1966	Senator	Robertson	59.4	44.0	59.0
1969	Governor	Battle*†	59.2	34.2	45.7
1969‡	Governor	Battle†	58.9	45.8	61.2

Sources: Adapted from tables 16 and 17 of J. Harvie Wilkinson III, *Harry Byrd and the Changing Face of Virginia Politics* (Charlottesville: University Press of Virginia, 1968), pp. 197–98. Election data for 1969 compiled from official election results provided by the State Board of Elections.

Note: For the bounds of the urban corridor, see fig. 1.

* The percentage votes for the two Battles are lower than those of other Organization candidates because there were three major candidates in 1969 and five major candidates in 1949. In all other elections listed in this table, there were but two major candidates.

† William C. Battle is listed as the Organization candidate even though another primary candidate, Fred G. Pollard, had the support of some elements of the Organization. For the runoff, however, almost all major Organization figures were supporting Battle.

‡ Runoff election for governor.

Chapter 11

The Future of
the Direct Primary in Virginia

It has been a long road for the Virginia primary since its auspicious inaugural in 1905. Advocated by Progressives but instituted by an Organization, the primary's history and development was intertwined with the fortunes of a political machine and the windfall from a restricted suffrage. In a very real sense, the primary was the vehicle for political control of the Old Dominion during most of the twentieth century. While it benefited one faction to the detriment of both the other faction and the Republican party, the primary nonetheless received broad-based support, reflecting origins that were at once democratic and oligarchic. But the forces unloosed by the federal courts and the federal Congress in its sixth decade brought ruin to the Virginia primary. Conservatives recoiled at a new liberal electorate which had stolen their control of the primary, and they forsook the house of their fathers. Liberals reconsidered their support of a nomination process which they surely owned but which helped to deliver few electoral prizes in the long run—indeed, a process which may have actually damaged their likelihood of a general election victory. Despite occasional lukewarm endorsements by many party leaders and the acknowledged support which it retains among some liberals, the Democratic party primary does not, at present, appear to possess a promising future. Statewide primaries—the 1977 gubernatorial primary is an example—may continue to be held sporadically as political conditions dictate. Some regions of Virginia may cling as tenaciously to the primary as the Southwest did to its convention while the latter was the party's nominating pariah. Although the primary may well prove to be more resilient than expected, the era of total primary domination of the Democratic nominating process has ended.

Its past shortcomings aside, is there a place for the primary in the party's future nominating structure? What role could and should the primary, or the convention, play in selecting candidates? What are the advantages and disadvantages of the various nomination methods from the perspective of the voter, the candidate, and the party itself? No final answers have ever been given to these weighty queries, and no ultimate solutions will be forthcoming from the analysis which follows.

Yet, some suggestions—which are admittedly only opinions—do appear reasonable, sound, justifiable, and plausible, and these will be offered.

The Modern Primary in the United States

The direct primary is a universal nominating tool in the United States, and every state holds a primary for at least some offices. Forty states were committed to its use for all statewide offices as of 1975.[1] Connecticut, and more recently New York and Delaware, do not use the statewide primary except in the case of a "challenge" to the party convention nominees. Elaborate statutory regulation of party primaries is the norm, but there are six exceptions, all southern states, of which Virginia is one.[2] This, of course, permits the Virginia Democratic party, as well as the state GOP, considerable flexibility in its nominating decisions. By party action alone, the primary can be abolished entirely or modified in countless ways. An effort to secure legislative approval of changes—which can be time-consuming and hazardous—is thus necessary. Further, Virginia is one of only four states—along with Georgia, Alabama, and South Carolina—which permit party officials to determine whether a primary or a convention is employed to nominate statewide candidates.[3]

There are three main varieties of the primary in use today. The "closed primary," which was found in forty states as of 1974,[4] requires a voter to openly declare his party choice and limits a voter's participation to this party's primary. In some states, but not Virginia,

[1] States legislate new primary regulations frequently, so the totals cited here and elsewhere in the text should be regarded only as approximates. The most current information can be found in the biennial *Book of the States*, though the data there often require clarification before use.

[2] The other southern states are Alabama, Arkansas, Georgia, North Carolina, and South Carolina. The latter originally regulated its primary to a much greater degree, but after the abolition of the "white primary" by the Supreme Court in 1944, South Carolina repealed all laws concerning the primary and party to give the widest possible latitude to the Democratic party's efforts to evade the court ruling.

[3] There is one statutory limitation on this power in Virginia; as of 1970 any incumbent running for reelection who was nominated in a primary for his current term can demand a primary to nominate the party candidate for the succeeding term. In South Carolina a statute also places one limitation on the parties: no convention, except one to select state senators, can make nominations unless the decision to use the convention method is reached by a ¾ vote of the total party central committee membership.

[4] The District of Columbia, Puerto Rico, and the Virgin Islands have also adopted the closed primary. In 1968, 43 states used the closed primary, indicating slight decline.

the voter registers by party before the primary. Actually, the only meaning-ful closed primary is one where the voter is forced to indicate his party preference in advance of the primary. By this definition, only about a third of the states have the closed primary. In Virginia, a voter merely states his political affiliation at the polls if more than one party is holding a primary.[5] The second type of primary is the "open primary," which eight states had adopted by 1974.[6] A voter casts his ballot without ever disclosing his party affiliation or preference. He is given ballots for every party as he enters the polling booth, but only one party's ballot may be marked and cast. Sorauf has noted that "there is not such a great or critical distinction between an open primary and a closed primary which permits a voter to change his party affiliation on the date of the primary by taking a vague and unenforceable pledge that he plans to support its candidates at the approaching election."[7] Still a third kind of primary is the "blanket primary," which has been characterized as the "free love primary."[8] For many years it was unique to the state of Washington, but Alaska has also recently adopted it. Not only does a voter not disclose party affiliation, he is free to vote in the primary of more than one party. The ballot itself is of an "aggregate party" form with all candi-dates of all parties listed under each office.

A few other comparative measures of primary election characteristics should be presented. Access to the ballot in most states (Virginia included) is predicated on receipt of filing fees, petitions, and voter signatures. Some states require no signatures of qualified voters, however, and a few (Colorado and New Mexico among them) automatically place on the ballot any candidate who receives at least a 20 percent endorse-ment vote at a state party convention. Cross-filing, whereby a candidate could simultaneously seek the nominations of both major parties, has not been permitted for statewide offices by any state since California abolished it in 1959.[9] Only eleven states—all southern and border—have

---

[5] Even when only one party holds a primary, a voter in Virginia could be challenged by any other voter or election judge until recently, as already reviewed. Most other states also have challenge provisions, although the specifics vary widely.

[6] Guam also uses the open primary. This category has registered a gain of three states (New Jersey, North Dakota, and Vermont) and the loss of one state (Alaska) since 1968. States using the open primary throughout the period since its adoption are Michigan, Minnesota, Montana, Utah, and Wisconsin.

[7] Sorauf, *Party Politics in America*, p. 205.

[8] Daniel M. Ogden, Jr., "The Blanket Primary and Party Regularity in Washington," *Pacific Northwest Quarterly* 39 (1948): 33–38.

[9] This novel system enabled Earl Warren to win the gubernatorial nominations of both major parties in 1946. New York State still has a semblance of this system thanks to its two "major" minor parties, the Conservatives and the Liberals.

ever employed a full-fledged runoff primary. Ten of these states still retain it. Interestingly, Virginia was not only the last of the eleven to adopt the runoff, it was the first to drop it, in a 1970 code revision.[10] Iowa has devised an intriguing alternative to the runoff; if no candidate receives 35 percent of the vote in the first primary, a party convention then selects the candidate. Finally, note should be made of the nonpartisan primary, which nominates the legislature of Nebraska and thousands of local officials and judges in other states as well. Informal party activity is common, however, even for candidates in areas where parties do not endorse. In most states the nonpartisan election is distinguished by the lack of party labels on the ballot. In the Old Dominion, though, no party designations appear on the ballot for any national, state, or local offices except presidential elections; so one might suggest that all Virginia elections are institutionally "nonpartisan."[11]

Even at its zenith, the direct primary did not totally eclipse the convention. Undoubtedly, the national party presidential conventions and the attendant state conventions helped to keep the system alive. Minor parties and the weaker party in the state (such as the GOP in Virginia) usually kept the convention nominating method when laws permitted them to do so. In some states where the primary began to dominate, a few officers continued to be selected by convention, and many states settled into a mixed pattern of primaries and conventions. Michigan, for example, nominates only candidates for governor in a primary, and Indiana selects only the state officer nominees by primary. Some states have also developed interesting combinations of the primary and convention methods which are used in nominating candidates for each office. As of 1975 preprimary "endorsing assemblies" are held in Colorado and preprimary conventions are held in Utah to endorse party favorites as a cue to party workers and members before and during the primary balloting. More than one candidate can be endorsed for each office in both states. In Utah each convention is required to designate the two candidates with the highest number of votes as endorsed primary candidates. No other candidate can file for the ballot, and voters are limited to the two choices selected by the convention. If one candi-

---

[10] The ten states besides Virginia which have maintained a runoff primary system are Alabama, Arkansas, Florida, Georgia, Louisiana, Mississippi, North Carolina, Oklahoma, Texas, and South Carolina. The District of Columbia, Guam, and Puerto Rico also have adopted the runoff. Tennessee's runoff, as earlier noted, was designed only to break an unlikely tie vote in a statewide contest.

[11] An excellent history and analysis of nonpartisan elections is contained in Willis D. Hawley, *Nonpartisan Elections and the Case for Party Politics* (New·York: John Wiley and Sons, 1973).

date receives 70 percent of the delegate vote, he is certified the
official candidate and does not run in the primary. Colorado's system
has been in effect continuously since 1912.[12] All candidates who poll more
than 20 percent of the convention vote are placed on the ballot, in the
order of their finish in the convention. This system returns the basic
authority and power of candidate selection to the party convention even
though a primary is held. As Hugh Bone reports:

> The conventions, called assemblies, have in reality designated nearly all of the
> party's candidates either because only a single candidate was named or because of
> the great advantage resulting from being listed first on the ballot. Without broad
> support within the assembly, prospective candidates are eliminated. Competition
> is markedly reduced in the primaries and for the Colorado House fewer than
> one-fourth of the primaries have been contested. In effect, primary contests
> are predetermined by assembly action, and primary elections serve a very limited
> purpose. In four primary elections for governor or United States senator, the
> average primary vote was only 20 percent.[13]

Idaho and Massachusetts also held preprimary conventions until 1974,
when both states adopted the full direct primary system. In Idaho under
the old convention system, candidates receiving 20 percent of the vote in
the convention were officially endorsed, although there must have been at
least two such candidates for each office. Only unendorsed candidates
who secured at least 10 percent of the vote could file and run in the
primary. Minnesota also has an optional preprimary endorsement, and the
Democratic-Farmer-Labor party (their version of the Democratic party)
has used it with a two-thirds vote of the convention delegates necessary
to make an endorsement.[14] Since 1960 the Republican party in Minnesota
has reversed its former opposition to this method of nomination, and
now endorses candidates who receive a 60 percent vote of its convention.
Endorsement is not noted on the ballot but is made known through sample
ballots and the press. Again, the parties appear to have reasserted
a large measure of Organizational control over the choice of candidates
by the use of this method. Between 1944 and 1960 about four-fifths
of the Minnesota Democratic-Farmer-Labor party's endorsees won the
primary nomination. One further variation of preprimary endorsement
should also be noted. In California parties themselves are forbidden by
statute to endorse primary candidates, so a system of designation by

[12] See R. John Eyre and Curtis Martin, *The Colorado Preprimary System* (Boulder: Bureau of Governmental Research and Service, University of Colorado, 1967).

[13] Hugh A. Bone, *American Politics and the Party System* (4th ed., New York: McGraw-Hill, 1971), p. 277.

[14] See G. Theodore Mitau, *Politics in Minnesota*, 2d ed. rev. (Minneapolis: University of Minnesota Press, 1970), pp. 68–71.

informal assemblies has developed.[15] The California Democratic Council and California Republican Assembly have had considerable influence on the primary election results in their respective parties, and many prospective candidates decide against filing if they fail to receive the endorsement of their party's extralegal group.

The most publicized and one of the most successful alternatives to the direct primary nominating system was devised by Connecticut, the site of the first recorded primary election in 1689. Known as the "challenge primary," it was adopted "without a conspicuous show of affection" in 1955 by the state which had resisted the modern primary longer than any other.[16] Basically, both parties nominate their candidates by conventions, and unless challenged by unsuccessful convention candidates, the nominees thus selected automatically appear on the general election ballot. The limitations on challenges are not severe, yet the requirements discourage them. A challenge can only be filed by someone who sought the nomination in convention, who secured support from at least 20 percent of the delegates, and who has filed necessary signatures, fees, and nominating petitions after the convention. There have rarely been challenges to convention nominees. For many years Connecticut stood alone in its support of the challenge primary, but two other states have recently adopted similar systems. In Delaware the structure is akin to that of Connecticut, but the number of potential primaries is reduced still further by the requirement that a candidate must have received at least 35 percent of the convention vote to register a challenge. New York introduced a challenge primary structure in 1970. Candidates for statewide offices are designated by the state central committee of each party. Anyone who receives at least 25 percent of the committee's votes may demand a primary. Additionally, a candidate who secures 20,000 signatures of qualified voters on a petition may require that a primary be held.[17]

Duane Lockard, who has written extensively on the mechanics and effects of the Connecticut challenge primary, has offered a convincing explanation both for the state's long delay in instituting any primary and for its eventual establishment of the unique challenge system:

[15] See Francis Carney, *The Rise of Democratic Clubs in California* (New York: McGraw-Hill, 1960); and Joseph P. Harris, *California Politics* (Stanford, Calif.: Stanford University Press, 1955).

[16] Sorauf, *Party Politics in America*, p. 209. The attention of scholars has been drawn to the Connecticut system by the research of Duane Lockard, *Connecticut's Challenge Primary: A Study in Legislative Politics* (New York: McGraw-Hill, 1960).

[17] In 1970 only 10,000 signatures were required to serve a primary, but this figure was doubled in 1974.

Why such protracted and successful resistance? Connecticut is not immune to political innovation. Although it may be known as "The Land of Steady Habits," it has nonetheless adopted an imposing array of progressive legislation, particularly in matters of labor law and social welfare. Still, matters of party concern are different—at least in Connecticut. For Connecticut parties are different from those of most other states; they are strong, centralized, and highly competitive with each other. The character of Connecticut party leadership—the power it has and the generally responsible manner in which it uses its power—constitutes the main reason why advocates of the primary made so little progress in Connecticut.[18]

The challenge primary, then, is a product of a strong and disciplined two-party system, and not incidentally works to reinforce that same system.

Weighing the relative merits and demerits of candidate selection processes can be a perplexing task. The interests of the voters, the candidates, the party leadership, and the party activists must all be taken into account, and what is good for one of these groups is often detrimental to another. The conclusion which any one individual deciding the "best" method of nomination would reach, then, would depend on that individual's perspective and his goals. In this discussion the varying nominating methods will be examined from the perspectives of all the affected groups with but one goal in mind: to determine a candidate selection process which will "impose a high degree of responsibility on a party organization for the selection of candidates yet keep open the channels of recruitment to qualified persons."[19]

The voter usually can be expected to urge the primary system of nomination, since his participation and influence is assured in a primary if he wishes to exercise his franchise. A convention normally involves only a select number of individuals, party workers primarily. The voter may also be inclined to support the open, rather than closed, primary. An open primary (and a blanket primary even more so) gives participants the widest possible choice, and they can cast their ballots in the contests which most interest them, regardless of party preference. They also are not publicly forced to disclose party affiliation. Yet, some members of the electorate note the increased burden which the primary, and particularly the open primary, places on their shoulders. They face a choice between many candidates for each office without the benefit of the party identification cues. As Sorauf surmised:

[18] Lockard, p. 1.
[19] Bone, p. 268.

For large numbers of voters in the primary the choice is more difficult than that at the general election. Since all of the candidates come from the same party, the voter's party loyalties cannot guide his decision. Nor can any reaction to "ins" and "outs." The primary campaign is brief, the candidates are not well-known, and the issues, if any, are often unclear. The voter's choice is, therefore, less well-structured and less predictable; the presence of an incumbent in the race may be the only continuing, stabilizing element. Consequently, many voter decisions are made right in the polling booth; the effect of the [first position on the ballot] and the success of the famous "names" indicate that. Small wonder, then, that parties are never confident in primaries and that public opinion pollers prefer not to predict primary outcomes.[20]

This added instability and uncertainty for voters contributes to the low turnouts which characterize primaries in two-party competitive states[21] and encourages nomination by an unrepresentative electorate, such as the one which has developed in Virginia primaries of late. The thoughtful voter will not likely favor these developments. But the convention method of nomination is not palatable to many concerned voters either. They would have an opportunity to influence the convention choice of party candidates only by a time-consuming commitment to the party as a precinct worker or other official, so that they could legitimately seek a delegate's berth at the convention. Their occupation or family responsibilities may not afford them the opportunity to do so, yet they may earnestly desire a voice in at least some nominations. A reasonable compromise might well be found in the institution of the preprimary party assemblies or a challenge primary. The party could provide the "cues" desired by many voters, and other undesirable characteristics of the primary—such as the low participation rate and the unrepresentative electorate which often results—might be altered somewhat in the process. The involvement of the party organization before the primary and the excitement and interest generated by the convention might actually increase turnout at the primary, should there be one, and help to make the distribution of primary votes more representative of the party constituency, and perhaps of the electorate as a whole. The party could have a major say in the nomination of its candidates, and the voter also usually would be permitted a voice in the process. The challenge primary would give the greater weight to the party, of course, since fewer primaries are likely to be held than under the preprimary endorsement plan. For that reason,

[20] Sorauf, *Party Politics in America*, p. 218.

[21] Low turnouts occur even in the two states which have the blanket primary, where the stimulus to participate would appear to be greatest for the individual voter. See Bone, pp. 268–69.

the voter might view the endorsement assembly as the optimal compromise from his perspective.

The candidate also gives the primary a mixed review. Direct primaries are as expensive as any other election and can drain financial contributors before the major battle in November. Often the candidate must also appeal, publicly and repeatedly, to an electorate of considerably different composition than the general electorate. The positions which he espouses in a primary may therefore be inappropriate for the general election and thus damaging to him in the long run. The bitterness which sometimes results from a primary can be disastrous, and the general election opposition may benefit directly from the charges and counter-charges which accompany intraparty warfare. But a primary can also give valuable campaign and organizational experience to an electoral novitiate. And the primary usually opens up the selection process to a larger number of people, including thousands who either are not directly involved in the internal affairs of the party or are out of favor with the current party leadership. Yet, conventions have a strong appeal for the candidate, too. They require a much smaller financial outlay and involve a campaign centered around a relatively limited number of party activists and workers. Dissension is usually more easily contained. But the candidate normally receives much less exposure to the broader base of voters and does not derive the benefits of "on the stump" campaign experience. And, clearly, a maverick is much less likely to be selected (although it could hardly be termed an impossible event). Many times the party leadership seek simply to reward loyal party service by bestowing nominations upon the faithful—actions which do much to strengthen the authority and security of the leadership itself. How can these conflicting testimonies be reconciled? Again, a logical and sensible solution can be found in a preprimary assembly or challenge primary. The candidate, theoretically at least, can have the best of both worlds, familiarizing himself with the interests and opinions of party activists, while usually participating (in the case of endorsing assemblies) in a popular election as well. The party may help to finance the endorsed candidate in the primary, thus partially relieving the personal financial burden. If the candidate is the overwhelming choice of party regulars, he is also spared a primary battle. If he is not the leadership favorite or cannot muster a convention majority for other reasons, but can still demonstrate a measure of support within the party, he is free to take his case to the larger primary electorate.

Virginia's primary, of course, facilitated the development of a political machine, but the opposite result occurred in many other states.

Regardless of the real effect of the primary's institution from place to place, one of the original purposes of primary advocates was to weaken party organization. U.S. Senator George W. Norris of Nebraska, for example, premised his deep belief in the direct primary on the fact that the primary "lessens party spirit. . . . Partisanship blinds not only the public official but the ordinary citizen and tends to lead him away from good government." E. E. Schattschneider asserted that Americans have concentrated more attention on the nominating process than have any other people, a condition which he termed the "hypertrophy of the nominating process." Duane Lockard carried this characterization further, suggesting that the "hypertrophy of nominating procedures is probably a basic cause of the atrophy of party organization."[22] There is little dispute among political scientists that the concentration of attention on one particular nominating process—the direct primary—has resulted in not inconsiderable damage to the efficient, effective, and proper functioning of political parties. Frank J. Sorauf summarized a half dozen major difficulties for the party which are directly traceable to the primary system:

For the party which wants to influence nominations the primary greatly escalates the costs of politics. Contesting a primary, or supporting candidates in one, is considerably more expensive than holding a convention.

The primary diminishes the power of the party organization to reward its faithful with nomination for public office. It thus makes less certain one of the rewards by which the party can induce service in its ranks.

By curbing party control over nominations the primary denies the party a powerful lever for assuring the loyalty of its office-holders to the party platform or program. For if the party cannot control or prevent the reelection of the maverick office-holder, it really has no effective sanction for enforcing loyalty to its programs. The power of European parties to deny renomination to their recalcitrant parliamentarians contributes substantially to their maintenance of party discipline in Parliament.

The primary permits the nomination of a man hostile to the party organization and leadership, opposed to their platforms or programs, or out of key with the public image the party wants to project—or all three! At the worst it may permit

[22] George W. Norris, "Why I Believe in the Direct Primary," *Annals of the American Academy of Political and Social Science* 106 (Mar. 1923): 23, quoted in Fred. I. Greenstein, *The American Party System and the American People* (2d ed., Englewood Cliffs, N.J.: Prentice-Hall, 1970), pp. 64–65n. Norris put the political philosophy he expressed in the quotation into personal practice, later becoming an Independent and winning reelection to the U.S. Senate on this nonparty basis. E. E. Schattschneider, *Party Government* (New York: Farrar and Rinehart, 1942), p. 99; Duane Lockard, *The Politics of State and Local Government* (New York: Macmillan, 1963), p. 194.

the nomination of a man under the party label who will be, intentionally or not, a severe embarrassment to it.

The nature of the primary creates the distinct possibility that the party will find itself saddled with an "unbalanced" ticket for the general election. In the hypothetical case of an electorate divided into X (50%), Y (30%), and Z (20%)—and let X, Y, and Z represent regions, races, religions, ethnic or national groups—the voters at the primary may select all or most of the candidates from X. (We are assuming considerable bloc voting, but that assumption, after all, lies at the base of party attempts to balance tickets.) Party leaders unquestionably would feel that a stronger ticket for the general election campaign would include a sprinkling of Y's and Z's.

Related is the fact that the primary may produce a "loser" for the party. The nominee may be a man who appeals to only a shade more than half of the dedicated 20 or 30 per cent of the electorate who votes in the party's primary. He may be a man of too limited an appeal—limited to an issue, a group, or an immoderate ideology—to win the support of the broader electorate of the general election. Beyond all of these specific threats is the more general fear that the primary exacerbates party rifts, splits, factions, feuds, or whatever the headline writers choose to call them. It pits party man against party man, party group against party group. . . . The resulting wounds are often deep and slow to heal. The cost to the health and strength of the party is considerable.[23]

All of this is not to say that the parties have been defenseless victims of the primary or that the party exerts no influence over the selection of candidates in a primary election. Actually, party leaders in Virginia and in most other states have long had a great impact in primary contests, and "informal slate-making by party leaders is far more prevalent than most citizens realize."[24] Competition is stifled or temporarily eliminated with the promise of "your turn will come" and with patronage positions. Even without the preprimary endorsing assemblies many state parties have provided money, organization, workers, and leadership to favored candidates.

By no means, however, is the primary nominating method the choice of party organizations. The convention is far more closely tailored to the needs and desires of the party itself. In a convention nominations can be more easily controlled by the leadership and the "balancing" of the ticket can be accomplished with less effort. A convention does not drain the party financially and also assists the party in rewarding its loyal workers and activists. In theory the doctrine of party responsibility is also better served by a convention, since it secures some degree of party influence over the actions of its officeholders.[25] The party convention will be inclined

[23] Sorauf, *Party Politics in America*, pp. 210–11.

[24] Bone, p. 274.

[25] Malcolm Jewell rated party cohesion in the Connecticut state legislature as one of the

to choose candidates who stand a reasonable chance of being elected in November. This means fewer mavericks will be nominated and, perhaps, fewer poorly qualified candidates. The convention delegates, it is often contended, have the best interests of the party at heart since their own fortunes are closely tied to their party's fate. The contrast with primary voters as a whole is a sharp and valid one. For example, a study of voters in two Wisconsin primaries indicated that primary participants were no more closely identified with their parties than the average voter in a general election who did not participate in the primaries.[26] The most commonly cited reason for voting in a primary was simply that it was the "duty of a good citizen," and no real interest in the affairs or welfare of the party per se was evidenced. Judson James recently summarized the most cogent convention arguments: "At its best, a party convention provides a confrontation of the diverse elements and the opportunity to make rational assessments of the candidates needed for general election victory; hopefully, better balanced, better coordinated, and more competitive tickets are selected through this process." Party leaders would almost unanimously agree that their party conventions more than meet this optional standard. Yet James hastened to add this warning in his evaluation of the convention method: "The recent experience of New York State Democrats with a state nominating convention has hardly been reassuring, however. The 1958 and 1962 meetings were disasters for the state ticket and promoted the later passage of a challenge primary bill that drastically reduced the significance of the remaining state committee endorsement convention. . . . A state nominating convention is very vulnerable to charges of restricting popular participation and its representative character is always open to doubt."[27]

The primary can offer a few advantages to the party, despite the harmful side effects recounted earlier. "New faces" and untapped talent can be recruited in the primary with greater ease. Often these individuals will be overlooked by parties too oriented to the criteria of past party service and intraparty status. In this fashion the primary serves to ensure a more open party and a more inclusive political system generally. A primary can also test the party's campaign apparatus, serving as a "dry run" election in preparation for November, whenever the party has endorsed a candidate and is aiding him organizationally. It

---

highest in the nation, suggesting some validity in the theory of a convention nomination's relationship to responsible party government.

[26] Austin Ranney and Leon D. Epstein, "The Two Electorates: Voters and Non-Voters in a Wisconsin Primary," *Journal of Politics* 28 (1966): 598–616.

[27] Judson L. James, *American Political Parties in Transition* (New York: Harper and Row, 1974), pp. 103–4.

cannot be denied, though, that a strong, disciplined party system does not usually mix with the primary nomination method.[28] And a vigorous party naturally abhors the open or blanket primary, both of which encourage "raiding" of a party's election by Independents or members of other parties.[29] The California Supreme Court, in upholding that state's first primary law which established a closed system, succinctly stated the parties' case for the closed primary:

If the indiscriminate right to vote with any party at a primary were given to electors, whether they were in accord with the principles of the party or not, it would soon tend to destroy all party organization. . . . A political party is an organization of electors believing in certain principles concerning governmental affairs and urging the adoption and execution of those principles through the election of their respective candidates at the polls. The existence of such parties lies at the foundation of our government and it is not expressing it too strongly to say that such parties are essential to its very existence.[30]

Virginia had a closed primary system, until 1976, when the statutory authorization for party rules closing the primary was replaced by a statute opening the primary to any registered voter. Even when the closed primary was in effect, however, it was never rigidly enforced and was openly violated frequently, sometimes with encouragement from elected leaders. Despite weaknesses in its operation in the Old Dominion, the closed primary appears clearly preferable to other systems from the important standpoint of party responsibility in candidate selection—which was one of two criteria established here for evaluating the various methods. It has also become clearer, as the perspectives of voter, then candidate, and finally party were examined, that either the challenge primary of Connecticut or preprimary endorsing assemblies like those of Colorado and Utah go further toward fulfilling both of the original goals—encouragement of party responsibility in the nomination process and maintenance of open channels of recruitment for qualified persons—than any other methods

[28] When the primary electorate is easily controlled, as in pre-1965 Virginia, a primary can match the needs of a political machine very well. But these conditions are not so easily arranged in the very different legal and political atmosphere prevailing in the 1970s.

[29] Raiding can also occur in closed primaries, too, especially in states where the loyalty challenge rather than party registration is the method used to check party affiliation at the polls (Bone, p. 271n). Some political scientists believe that the structure of open primaries and especially blanket primaries may increase the incidence of raiding, but at least one study suggests that this may not be so in practice; see Daniel M. Ogden, Jr., "Washington's Popular Primary," *Research Studies of Washington State College* 19 (1951): 139–61.

[30] *Socialist Party* v. *Uhl*, 155 Cal. 793 (1909), quoted in Goodman, p. 131.

examined. On the one hand, the pure primary system does little to sustain the party organization and does a good deal to damage it by denying the party a fundamental power: "The making of nominations is the one political decision the American party makes as a political organization. The electorate decides the general election. If one deprives the party organization of the power to nominate, the party is deprived of one of its few *raisons d'être* as a political party. Ultimately, the organization, stripped of one of its most meaningful tasks, will be weakened."[31] On the other hand, a convention system alone encourages control by a party elite in many cases and removes all basic control of the nominating process from the hands of the electorate. Neither pure system is satisfactory. The combination of systems inherent in the endorsing assembly or the challenge primary is more adequate; the party is given a major role in the selection of the candidates for which it will be responsible and the electorate is given an opportunity to voice its opinion on occasion and rebuke the party leadership if necessary.[32] It may well be that endorsing assemblies are preferable to the challenge primary because they more frequently involve a primary contest. In the case of Connecticut, Lockard noted that the challenge primary system produced only eighty-five actual primaries out of 1,600 potential elections in the period from 1955 to 1958. And in only six of thirty-four primaries surveyed during the same period did nonendorsed candidates oust endorsed candidates.[33] Connecticut's unique party competitive system is partially responsible for this result, no doubt. A state without a high degree of party discipline, like Virginia, would almost certainly observe a higher incidence of challenge primaries. Yet, the preprimary endorsing assemblies usually ensure a primary when real competition does indeed exist. The Utah system selects the two primary competitors for each office in party conventions; as long as at least two candidates run, a primary contest is assured. Only when one candidate pulls a landslide convention vote (70 percent or more) is a primary aborted entirely. The Colorado system appears to be an even sounder one from the primary's perspective, since all candidates who poll at least 20 percent of the convention vote are placed on the primary ballot. As many as five candidates, then, could contest each office in a primary, although the number of

[31] Frank J. Sorauf, *Political Parties in the American System* (Boston: Little, Brown and Company, 1964), p. 107.

[32] The New York State Democratic primaries of 1974 provide an excellent example of this "rebuking" power. The entire party-selected gubernatorial slate headed by Howard Samuels was soundly rejected by three unendorsed candidates. Samuels was defeated by Congressman Hugh Carey, who eventually was elected governor in November.

[33] Lockard, *Connecticut's Challenge Primary*, p. 24.

contestants is naturally lower in most cases. But the party also receives an added advantage in the primary since candidates are listed in order of their convention finish. Not only is the first ballot position valuable in general,[34] but it then serves as a party "cue" for voters. This added weight for parties, plus insurance for voters that a primary will be held whenever competition requires it, recommends highly the preprimary endorsing assemblies. The National Municipal League has long advocated the preprimary convention with party endorsements noted on the primary ballot.[35] The Committee on Political Parties of the American Political Science Association concurred with the conclusions reached by the Municipal League.[36] Scholars have agreed that the Colorado system, in particular, has had a beneficial effect on party organization and activity because "designations are denied to nonentities, and candidates expecting to make a serious bid for nomination must solicit and obtain support from party activists. . . . The [preprimary] convention links local committees with the state organizations and thereby probably reduces organizational atrophy."[37]

It is possible, then, in Virginia and in other states to temper the excesses of both primary and convention and to construct a nominating process which satisfies the most important needs and desires of the voter, the candidate, and the party. Suggested here for the consideration of both parties is a nominating method which appears to meet the criteria of party responsibility and ballot accessibility. That method is a form or variation of the preprimary endorsing assembly or the challenge primary. This system is not perfect, and flaws are apparent from many vantage points. Yet it is, at heart, a compromise of pure systems—the primary and the convention—neither of which has served or likely will serve Virginia eminently well by itself. The defects in the Commonwealth's direct primary have been exposed throughout this study. Grievances against the primary by the state's political right, left, and middle have accumulated—intensified by the fast-moving events of the last

[34] See Henry M. Bain and Donald S. Hecock, *Ballot Position and Voter's Choice: The Arrangement of Names on the Ballot and Its Effect on the Voter's Choice* (Detroit: Wayne State University Press, 1956).

[35] National Municipal League, Committee on Direct Primary, *A Model Direct Primary Election System* (New York: National Municipal League, 1951). See especially pp. 20–33, which contain a thorough presentation of the arguments supporting and opposing the preprimary party endorsement system. Other features of the league's primary plan include the mandatory use of the primary for all parties polling 10 percent or more of the vote at the preceding election and several provisions to ensure the possibility of candidacy for those not endorsed by parties.

[36] Key, *Politics, Parties, and Pressure Groups*, p. 394.

[37] Bone, p. 278.

decade—and threaten to deprive the primary of a significant role in the state's nominating process. But conventions alone are no panacea. The primary has a place in the future of Virginia's political parties, as a prominent component of a comprehensive and reinvigorated nominating system. The primary in the Old Dominion can adapt to the changing conditions which its benefactor, the Byrd machine, could not accommodate. Unlike the Organization, the Virginia primary does not have to become a political museum piece.

Appendixes
Bibliography
Index

Appendix I

Virginia's Congressional Districts, 1952–72

Virginia's Congressional Districts, 1952

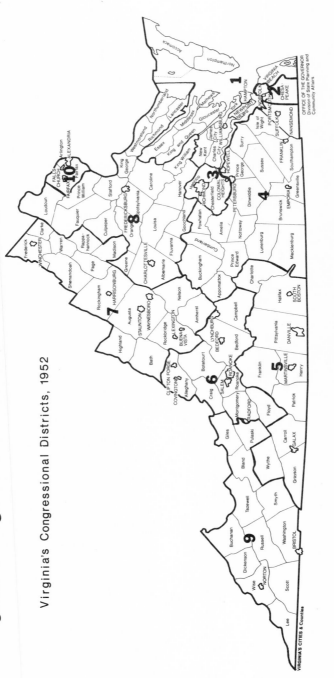

Source: Acts and Joint Resolutions of the General Assembly of the Commonwealth of Virginia (Regular Session, 1952), p. 1349. The base map was provided by the Division of State Planning and Community Affairs.

Virginia's Congressional Districts, 1965

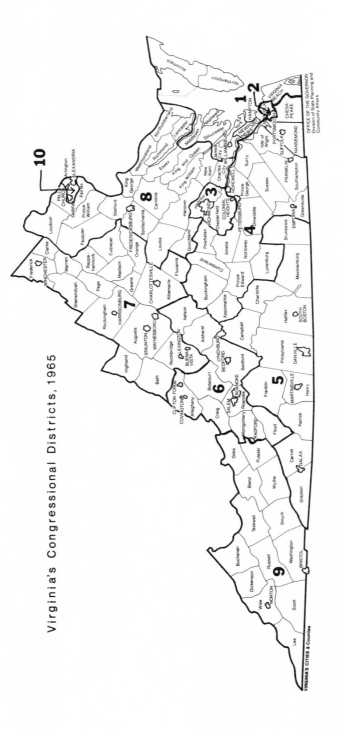

Source: Acts and Joint Resolutions of the General Assembly of the Commonwealth of Virginia (Extra Session, 1965), p. 1629. The base map was
provided by the Division of State Planning and Community Affairs.

Virginia's Congressional Districts, 1972

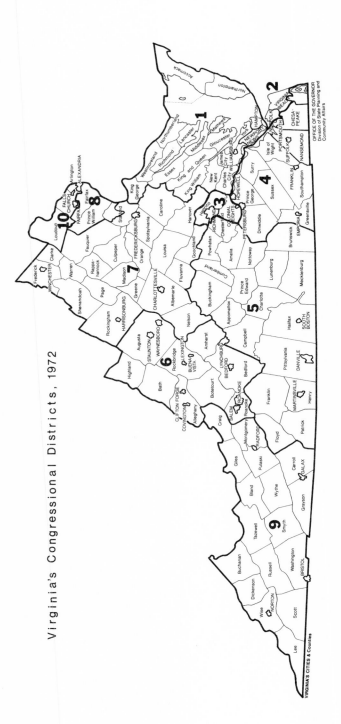

Source: Acts and Joint Resolutions of the General Assembly of the Commonwealth of Virginia (Regular Session, 1972), p. 1665. The base Map was provided by the Division of State Planning and Community Affairs.

Appendix II

Declaration of the 1899 May Movement

Richmond, Virginia, May 10, 1899
(Unanimously Adopted)

. . . We, members of the Democratic party, assembled in conference, reaffirming our devotion to the doctrines of the party and our fealty to its organization, do declare as follows:

1. We earnestly favor an amendment of the Federal Constitution, so that United States senators shall be elected by a direct vote of the people of the several States, instead of by the legislature thereof.

2. In the effort to secure such amendment, we invite the co-operation and assistance, not only of the people of Virginia, but the people of other states, whose welfare is equally involved.

3. Pending the adoption of such constitutional amendment, we favor the nomination of our party candidates for the United States Senate by State primary elections, or State conventions, and we ask the General Assembly for legislation legalizing such primaries whenever held.

4. We urgently and respectfully appeal to the State Central Democratic Committee to provide at once for holding a State primary or a State convention for the nomination of a Democratic candidate for the United States Senate to be voted for by the next General Assembly. . . .

5. In advance of action by the Central Committee, or in case it decline to act as recommended, we appeal to the Democratic voters of each legislative district to nominate no man for the next General Assembly unless he favors the principles herein expressed and pledges himself to support for the United States Senate a candidate who is the open and unequivocal advocate thereof. . . .

6. We now and here organize a Democratic League for Reform in the Election of United States Senators, to consist of members of this conference and all other Virginia Democrats who approve this declaration of principles. . . .

Source: Partial text of the Resolution of the Democratic Conference Advocating Popular Nomination and Election of U.S. Senators, Richmond *Dispatch*, May 11, 1899.

Democratic Primary Elections for Governor, Lieutenant Governor, and Attorney General in Virginia, 1905–73

Year	Office	Candidates	Vote for candidates	Percentage for candidates
1905	Governor	*Claude A. Swanson	42,638	51.2
		William H. Mann	20,485	24.6
		Joseph E. Willard	20,083	24.2
		Total	83,206	100.0
	Lieutenant governor	*J. Taylor Ellyson	69,758	79.2
		J. Alston Cabell	18,365	20.8
		Total	88,123	100.0
	Attorney general	*William A. Anderson	48,940	61.4
		Samuel W. Williams	30,767	38.6
		Total	79,707	100.0
1909	Governor	*William Hodges Mann	39,281	53.5
		Harry St. George Tucker	34,203	46.5
		Total	73,484	100.0
	Lieutenant governor	*J. Taylor Ellyson	49,556	69.1
		James R. Caton	22,168	30.9
		Total	71,724	100.0
	Attorney general	*Samuel W. Williams	46,236	65.4
		Robert Catlett	24,512	34.6
		Total	70,748	100.0
1913	Governor	Henry Carter Stuart	unopposed	
	Lieutenant governor[a]	*J. Taylor Ellyson	47,516	61.2
		Lewis H. Machen	28,275	36.4
		Alexander J. Wedderburn	1,880	2.4
		Total	77,671	100.0

Appendix III (*cont.*)

Year	Office	Candidates	Vote for candidates	Percentage for candidates
	Attorney general	Samuel W. Williams	31,202	45.4
		*John Garland Pollard	32,286	47.0
		S. Gordon Cumming	5,242	7.6
		Total	68,739	100.0
1917	Governor	*Westmoreland Davis	39,318	43.9
		J. Taylor Ellyson	27,811	31.1
		John Garland Pollard	22,436	25.0
		Total	89,565	100.0
	Lieutenant governor	B. F. Buchanan	unopposed	
	Attorney general	*John R. Saunders	45,517	53.8
		Hugh A. White	39,079	46.2
		Total	84,596	100.0
1921	Governor	*E. Lee Trinkle	86,812	57.6
		Harry St. George Tucker	64,286	42.4
		Total	150,669	100.0
	Lieutenant governor	*Junius E. West	55,997	41.0
		Julien Gunn	44,560	32.6
		Kenneth N. Gilpin	30,583	22.4
		William B. Fitzhugh	5,544	4.0
		Total	136,684	100.0
	Attorney general	John R. Saunders	unopposed	
1925	Governor	*Harry F. Byrd, Sr.	107,317	61.4
		G. Walter Mapp	67,579	38.6
		Total	174,896	100.0
	Lieutenant governor	Junius E. West	unopposed	
	Attorney general	*John R. Saunders	124,944	75.1
		Marvin Smithey	41,508	24.9
		Total	166,452	100.0

Appendix III (*cont.*)

Year	Office	Candidates	Vote for candidates	Percentage for candidates
1929	Governor	*John Garland Pollard	104,310	75.4
		G. Walter Mapp	29,386	21.3
		Rosewell Page	4,557	3.3
		Total	138,253	100.0
	Lieutenant governor	James H. Price	unopposed	
	Attorney general	John R. Saunders	unopposed	
1933	Governor	*George C. Peery	116,837	61.6
		J. T. Deal	40,268	21.2
		W. Worthsmith	32,518	17.2
		Total	189,623	100.0
	Lieutenant governor	James H. Price	unopposed	
	Attorney general	John R. Saunders	unopposed	
1937	Governor	*James H. Price	16,319	86.1
		Vivian L. Page	26,955	13.9
		Total	193,274	100.0
	Lieutenant governor	*Saxon W. Holt	109,259	56.7
		Robert W. Daniel	83,532	43.3
		Total	192,791	100.0
	Attorney general	*Abram P. Staples	102,727	54.8
		John Galleher	77,101	41.2
		W. Worth Smith, Jr.	7,503	4.0
		Total	187,331	100.0
1941	Governor	*Colgate W. Darden, Jr.	105,655	76.6
		Vivian L. Page	19,526	14.1
		Hunsdon Cary	12,793	9.3
		Total	137,974	100.0
	Lieutenant governor	*William M. Tuck	108,189	81.3
		Moss A. Plunkett	24,863	18.7
		Total	133,052	100.0
	Attorney general	Abram P. Staples	unopposed	

Appendix III (*cont.*)

Year	Office	Candidates	Vote for candidates	Percentage for candidates
1945	Governor	*William M. Tuck	97,304	70.1
		Moss A. Plunkett	41,484	29.9
		Total	138,788	100.0
	Lieutenant governor[b]	*Lewis Preston Collins	51,350	37.8
		Charles R. Fenwick	51,922	38.3
		Leonard G. Muse	32,426	23.9
		Total	135,698	100.0
	Attorney general	Abram P. Staples	unopposed	
1949[c]	Governor	*John Stewart Battle	135,436	42.8
		Francis P. Miller	111,697	35.3
		Remmie L. Arnold	22,054	7.0
		Horace H. Edwards	47,435	15.0
		Total	316,622	100.0
	Lieutenant governor	*Lewis Preston Collins	193,641	68.1
		Nick Prillaman	90,621	31.9
		Total	284,262	100.0
	Attorney general	*J. Lindsay Almond, Jr.	188,642	66.8
		Moss A. Plunkett	93,926	33.2
		Total	282,568	100.0
1953	Governor	*Thomas B. Stanley	150,499	65.9
		Charles R. Fenwick	77,715	34.1
		Total	228,214	100.0
	Lieutenant governor	*A. E. S. Stephens	150,735	75.1
		Charles Nicholas Loving	50,057	24.9
		Total	200,792	100.0
	Attorney general	J. Lindsay Almond, Jr.	unopposed	
1957	Governor	*J. Lindsay Almond, Jr.	119,307	79.5
		Howard H. Carwile	30,794	20.5
		Total	150,101	100.0
	Lieutenant governor	A. E. S. Stephens	unopposed	
	Attorney general[d]	Howard C. Gilmer, Jr.	unopposed	

Appendix III (*cont.*)

Year	Office	Candidates	Vote for candidates	Percentage for candidates
1961	Governor	* Albertis S. Harrison, Jr.	199,519	56.7
		A. E. S. Stephens	152,639	43.3
		Total	352,158	100.0
	Lieutenant governor	* Mills E. Godwin, Jr.	187,660	54.4
		Armistead L. Boothe	157,176	45.6
		Total	344,836	100.0
	Attorney general	* Robert Y. Button	178,134	51.9
		T. Munford Boyd	150,755	43.9
		Eugene C. Adkins	14,236	4.2
		Total	343,125	100.0
1965	Governor	Mills E. Godwin, Jr.	unopposed	
	Lieutenant governor	Fred G. Pollard	unopposed	
	Attorney general	Robert Y. Button	unopposed	
1969	Governor	* William C. Battle	158,956	38.9
		Henry E. Howell, Jr.	154,617	37.8
		Fred G. Pollard	95,057	23.3
		Total	408,630	100.0
	Lieutenant governor	* J. Sargeant Reynolds	242,085	63.9
		W. Carrington Thompson	89,765	23.7
		Herman "Hardtimes" Hunt	27,088	7.2
		Moses A. Riddick, Jr.	19,672	5.2
		Total	378,610	100.0
	Attorney general	* Andrew P. Miller	151,991	41.2
		Guy O. Farley, Jr.	129,241	35.0
		Bernard Levin	47,003	12.7
		C. F. Hicks	41,084	11.1
		Total	369,319	100.0
1969	Governor (Runoff)°	* William C. Battle	226,108	52.1
		Henry E. Howell, Jr.	207,505	47.9
		Total	433,613	100.0

Appendix III *(cont.)*

Year	Office	Candidates	Vote for candidates	Percentage for candidates
	Attorney general	*Andrew P. Miller	257,622	63.2
		Guy O. Farley, Jr.	150,140	36.8
		Total	407,762	100.0
1973	Governor[f]	(no nominee)		
	Lieutenant governor	J. Harry Michael, Jr.	unopposed	
	Attorney general	Andrew P. Miller	unopposed	

Sources: For all elections for governor before 1925, two sources were used: the *Annual Reports of the Secretary of the Commonwealth to the Governor and General Assembly* and the reports of the canvass by Democratic party officials as listed in state newspapers. Neither of these sources contained a complete accounting of each election; thus, considerable cross-referencing was necessary. These two sources were also used to determine the primary results for the office of lieutenant governor and attorney general from 1925 to 1933, inclusive. From the election of 1925 on, official state election results for governor as published by the State Board of Elections were used. From the election of 1937 on, official state election results for lieutenant governor and attorney general as published by the State Board of Elections were used.

Note: Before the election of 1929, several other statewide officers—including state corporation commissioners, secretary of the Commonwealth, superintendent of public instruction, treasurer, and commissioner of agriculture—were elected by primary vote. The "short ballot" reform, introduced during the administration of Governor Harry F. Byrd, Sr., limited the popular election of statewide officers to three: governor, lieutenant governor, and attorney general. Only votes for these three offices are included in this table.

*Denotes primary winner.

[a] Alexander J. Wedderburn withdrew his name from the contest eight days before the primary ballot, too late to remove his name from the ballot. The Richmond *News Leader* commented on July 30, 1913: "Mr. Wedderburn never was conceded to have any strength in the campaign and it is doubtful if his announced withdrawal will have any effect on the balloting one way or another."

[b] Despite official results which showed Charles R. Fenwick the primary winner, the election was awarded to L. Preston Collins by court order in a case involving ballot fraud (see pp. 55–56).

[c] The Republican party also held a statewide primary election—their first and only such primary—on the same day as the Democratic primary in 1949. Walter Johnson was unopposed for the gubernatorial nomination and received 8,888 votes. E. Thomas McGuire defeated Berkeley Williams with 4,635 votes (54.1 percent) to 3,930 votes (45.9 percent). No candidate filed for the Republican nomination for attorney general.

[d] Howard C. Gilmer, Jr., the Byrd Organization's choice for attorney general, withdrew before the primary, but his name remained on the ballot, and legally, no other candidate could file for the primary (see p. 68). A large write-in vote (1,065) was cast in the

Appendix III (*cont.*)

---

attorney general primary, with 700 votes for state Senator Albertis S. Harrison, Jr., 283 for Delegate Robert Whitehead, and 82 ballots for others.
ᵉ In the aftermath of anti-Organization candidate Francis Miller's near victory in the four-way gubernatorial primary in 1949, the Byrd Organization secured legislation permitting a primary runoff election in the event no candidate received a majority of the votes in the first primary. The runoff mechanism was not used until 1969, when it was requested by the runners-up in the gubernatorial and attorney general contests.
ᶠ Independent gubernatorial candidate Henry Howell received the "commendation" of the Democratic State Central Committee but was not the official nominee of the party.

Appendix IV

Democratic Primary Elections for U.S. Senate in Virginia, 1905–72

Year	Candidates	Vote for candidates	Percentage for candidates
1905	*Thomas S. Martin	46,691	56.3
	Andrew J. Montague	36,307	43.7
	Total	82,998	100.0
1909	John W. Daniel	unopposed	
1911	*Thomas S. Martin	65,18	67.5
	William A. Jones	31,428	32.5
	Total	96,646	100.0
1911 (special)	*Claude A. Swanson	67,497	70.1
	Carter Glass	28,757	29.9
	Total	96,254	100.0
1916	Claude A. Swanson	unopposed	
1918	Thomas S. Martin	unopposed	
1920 (special)	Carter Glass	unopposed	
1922	*Claude A. Swanson	102,045	73.0
	Westmoreland Davis	37,671	27.0
	Total	139,716	100.0
1924	Carter Glass	unopposed	
1928	Claude A. Swanson	unopposed	
1930	Carter Glass	unopposed	
1933 (special)	Harry F. Byrd, Sr.	unopposed	
1934	Harry F. Byrd, Sr.	unopposed	
1936	Carter Glass	unopposed	
1940	Harry F. Byrd, Sr.	unopposed	
1942	Carter Glass	unopposed	
1946[a]	*Harry F. Byrd, Sr.	141,923	63.5
	Martin Hutchinson	81,605	36.5
	Total	223,528	100.0
1948	*A. Willis Robertson	80,340	70.3
	James P. Hart, Jr.	33,928	29.7
	Total	114,268	100.0
1952	*Harry F. Byrd, Sr.	216,438	62.7
	Francis Pickens Miller	128,869	37.3
	Total	345,307	100.0

Appendix IV (*cont.*)

Year	Candidates	Vote for candidates	Percentage for candidates
1954	A. Willis Robertson	unopposed	
1958	Harry F. Byrd, Sr.	unopposed	
1960	A. Willis Robertson	unopposed	
1964	Harry F. Byrd, Sr.	unopposed	
1966	A. Willis Robertson	216,274	49.9
	*William B. Spong, Jr.	216,885	50.1
	Total	433,159	100.0
1966 (special)	*Harry F. Byrd, Jr.	221,221	50.9
	Armistead L. Boothe	212,996	49.1
	Total	434,217	100.0
1970	*George C. Rawlings, Jr.	58,874	45.7
	Clive L. DuVal, 2d	58,174	45.1
	Milton Colvin	11,911	9.2
	Total	128,959	100.0
1972	William B. Spong, Jr.	unopposed	

Sources: For all primary elections for U.S. Senate before 1948, two sources were used: *The Annual Reports of the Secretary of the Commonwealth to the Governor and General Assembly* and the reports of the canvass by Democratic party officials as listed in state newspapers. For primary elections for the U.S. Senate from 1948 on, official results provided by the State Board of Elections were used.

Note: The first Democratic primary election for U.S. Senate was held in 1905. U.S. senators were still formally elected by the state legislature, which was elected in odd-numbered years in Virginia. The Seventeenth Amendment to the U.S. Constitution was ratified in 1913, and thereafter U.S. senators were elected by popular vote in November of even-numbered years.

* Denotes primary winner.

ᵃ Incumbent Carter Glass died in 1946, and Democrats held a state convention to nominate a candidate for the remaining two years of his term. Congressman A. Willis Robertson won the nomination, defeating Congressman Howard W. Smith.

Appendix V

Methods of Nomination for the Virginia General Assembly, 1923-75

Year	Democratic Party			Number of seats contested by Republican Party in November[a]
	Contested primary	Uncontested primary	Convention	
1975*	28	42	62	68
1973	3	48	31	60
1971*	45	45	44	98
1969	36	N.A.	N.A.	55
1967*	54	61	21	78
1965*	64	53	19	64
1963*	36	82	20	49
1961	30	N.A.	N.A.	27
1959*	46	N.A.	N.A.	23
1957	27	N.A.	N.A.	34
1955*	42	N.A.	N.A.	28
1953	41	43	15	33
1951*	51	N.A.	N.A.	39
1949	46	39	14	23
1947*	56	N.A.	N.A.	33
1945	25	55	18	11
1943*	46	N.A.	N.A.	16
1941	31	N.A.	N.A.	14
1939*	57	N.A.	N.A.	22
1937	38	43	14	20
1935*	64	62	14	25
1933	66	18	16	18
1931*	54	N.A.	N.A.	19
1929	34	43	23	76[b]
1927*	75	44	20	N.A.
1923*	66	53	21	N.A.

Sources: Reports carried in state newspapers served as source material for this table. Election accounts from several Virginia newspapers were cross-referenced to provide this information; yet some inaccuracies undoubtedly exist due to incomplete news reports and errors by the author in tabulation, especially in the earlier years listed in this table. In addition, reliable figures on the number of candidates nominated by conventions and unopposed primaries were not available from any source in about a third of the years surveyed.

Note: Information from source materials was sketchy and unreliable for the year 1925 and years before 1923, although primary elections for the General Assembly have been held in many parts of Virginia since the institution of the first statewide Democratic primary in 1905. In some cities and counties of Virginia, General Assembly primaries were even held for several years before 1905. During the years surveyed, the Republican party held primary elections for legislative seats only in 1949, 1965, 1969, 1973, and 1975. In this table only regular elections for the General Assembly are surveyed, with the exception of the special state Senate election in 1965, where court-ordered redistricting resulted in a new election for all 40 seats. The figures in this table represent the number of legislative seats nominated by various methods. Each seat in the General Assembly was counted as one unit. In a few cases throughout the years surveyed, no candidate would file for a seat. In such instances local party committees would sometimes nominate a candidate. These cases are not included in any of the three nominating categories in this table.

* Denotes years in which elections were held for both the House of Delegates and state Senate. Only the House of Delegates was elected in unstarred election years. Total membership of the House is 100 and of the Senate is 40.

N.A.: Not available.

ᵃ Almost all Republican nominations were made by the convention method, which has traditionally been used by the Republican party in all areas of the state except Northern Virginia. A few nominations for these seats were filled in uncontested primaries, found primarily in Northern Virginia during the 1960s and 1970s.

ᵇ The number of "Republican" candidates for the General Assembly was greatly inflated in 1929 by the addition of the "Coalitionist" Democratic-Republican candidates. Many of the "Coalitionist" candidates running with Republican support were Democrats opposed to the policies of the 1928 Democratic presidential nominee "Al" Smith. The "Coalitionists" won only eight seats and were a phenomenon of this election only.

Appendix VI

Democratic Primary Elections for the Virginia General Assembly, by Regions, 1923–75

Number of Primary Elections Held in Region[a]

Year	Northern Virginia	Piedmont	Northern Neck–Eastern Shore	Richmond	Hampton Roads	Tidewater excluding H.R.	Southside	Southwest	West	Shenandoah Valley	Total no. for year
1975*	4	1	1	3	4	0	0	0	0	0	13
1973	1	0	0	0	0	0	1	0	0	0	2
1971*	6	1	2	2	3	0	4	0	0	0	18
1969	3	1	0	2	2	0	4	2	0	0	14
1967*	2	1	2	3	9	0	4	1	2	0	24
1965*	6	4	2	1	6	0	4	1	2	1	27
1963*	2	4	2	3	3	0	1	0	4	0	19
1961	1	3	1	4	2	1	3	0	1	0	16
1959*	3	2	3	2	9	1	2	0	2	0	24
1957	4	4	0	1	2	0	2	0	0	0	13
1955*	4	6	3	2	5	0	5	0	4	0	29
1953	3	5	4	2	3	1	4	1	2	0	25
1951*	2	5	3	4	7	0	7	0	4	1	33
1949	2	7	5	1	4	0	9	0	4	1	33

Appendix VI (cont.)

Number of Primary Elections Held in Region[a]

Year	Northern Virginia	Piedmont	Northern Neck–Eastern Shore	Richmond	Hampton Roads	Tidewater excluding H.R.	Southside	Southwest	West	Shenandoah Valley	Total no. for year
1947*	6	9	2	2	7	1	5	0	4	1	37
1945	3	2	0	1	2	0	4	0	0	1	13
1943*	3	6	2	2	4	0	7	0	4	0	28
1941	2	6	3	1	2	1	5	0	0	0	20
1939*	2	7	4	3	9	1	9	0	4	1	40
1937	1	5	3	3	5	2	3	2	1	0	25
1935*	3	12	7	5	6	2	9	3	4	1	52
1933	2	11	6	2	8	3	12	1	7	2	54
1931*	2	10	6	2	7	3	14	0	3	0	47
1929	1	3	4	2	2	1	2	0	1	0	16
1927*	2	9	5	4	8	4	9	0	4	1	46
1923*	3	11	6	4	6	4	8	2	5	0	49
Total	73	135	76	61	126	25	137	13	62	10	717

Sources: Reports carried in state newspapers served as source material for this table. Election accounts from several Virginia newspapers were cross-referenced to provide this information; yet some inaccuracies undoubtedly exist due to incomplete news reports and errors by the author in tabulation, especially in the earlier years listed in this table.

Note: Information from source materials was sketchy and unreliable for the year 1925 and years before 1923, although primary elections for the

Table VI (*cont.*)

General Assembly have been held in many parts of Virginia since the institution of the first statewide Democratic primary in 1905. In some cities and counties of Virginia, General Assembly primaries had even been held for several years before 1905. During the years surveyed, the **Republican** party held primary elections for legislative seats only in 1949, 1965, 1969, 1973, and 1975. All of these primaries were held in the **Northern** Virginia regional area, except in 1949, when the city of Norfolk and Bedford County as well as Fairfax County had GOP primaries. In this table only regular elections for the General Assembly are surveyed, with the exception of the special state Senate election in 1965, where court-ordered redistricting resulted in a new election for all 40 seats. For exact definition of the regions of Virginia, see fig. 1.

* Denotes years in which elections were held for both the House of Delegates and state Senate. Only the House of Delegates was elected in unstarred election years. Total membership of the House is 100 and of the Senate is 40.

ᵃ The figures entered in this table represent the number of primary elections held, not the number of seats contested in primaries. For example, a primary held in a multimember House district in a given year is counted as one primary election, even though several seats are contested in the district. When a House or Senate district crossed regional lines, it was included in the region which contained a majority of the district's population.

Bibliography

Public Documents, State

Attorney General of Virginia. *Report of the Attorney General to the Governor of Virginia, 1900 [-1935]*. Richmond: Department of State Printing, 1900 [-1935].

Opinions of the Attorney General and Report to the Governor of Virginia, 1936 [-1975]. Richmond: Department of Purchases and Supply, 1936 [-1975].

General Assembly of Virginia. *Acts and Joint Resolutions of the General Assembly of the Commonwealth of Virginia, 1888 [-1975]*. Richmond: Department of Purchases and Supply, 1888 [-1975]. Regular and Special Sessions.

Manual of the Senate and House of Delegates, 1955 [-1975]. Richmond: Department of Purchases and Supply, 1955 [-1975].

Secretary of the Commonwealth. *Annual Report of the Secretary of the Commonwealth to the Governor and General Assembly of Virginia, 1900 [-1930]*. Richmond: Department of State Printing, 1900 [-1930].

State Board of Elections. *Statement of the Vote, 1927 [-1974]*. Richmond: Department of Purchases and Supply, 1927 [-1974].

____. *Virginia Election Laws, As Amended to 1974 [-1975]*. (Code of Virginia, Title 24.1). Richmond: Department of Purchases and Supply, 1974 [-1975].

____. "Estimated Number of Registered Voters in Virginia, 1957 [-1964]." Mimeographed. Richmond: State Board of Elections, 1957 [-1964].

Virginia Democratic Party. *The Party Plan, 1971 [-1975]*. Richmond: Democratic Party State Central Committee, 1971 [-1975].

Public Documents, National

Congressional Quarterly, Inc. *Guide to U.S. Elections*. Washington, D.C.: Congressional Quarterly, 1975.

Congressional Research Service, Library of Congress. *The Constitution of the United States of America: Analysis and Interpretation*. Washington, D.C.: U.S. Government Printing Office, 1973.

U.S. Bureau of the Census. *County and City Data Book, 1972*. Washington, D.C.: U.S. Government Printing Office, 1973.

Statistical Abstract of the United States, 1971. 92d ed. Washington, D.C.: U.S. Government Printing Office, 1971.

Census of Population 1970, General Population Characteristics: Final Report PC(1)-B48, Virginia. Washington, D.C.: U.S. Government Printing Office, 1971.

Books

Bain, Henry M., and Donald S. Hecock. *Ballot Position and Voter's Choice: The Arrangement of Names on the Ballot and Its Effect on the Voter's Choice.* Detroit: Wayne State University Press, 1956.

Beckett, Paul. *The Direct Primary in New Mexico.* Albuquerque: Department of Government, University of New Mexico, 1947.

Beman, Lamar Taney. *The Direct Primary.* New York: H. W. Wilson Company, 1926.

Berman, David R. *State and Local Politics.* Boston: Holbrook Press, 1975.

Bone, Hugh A. *American Politics and the Party System.* 4th ed. New York: McGraw-Hill, 1971.

Buni, Andrew. *The Negro in Virginia Politics, 1902-1965.* Charlottesville: University Press of Virginia, 1967.

Campbell, Angus, et al. *The American Voter.* New York: John Wiley and Sons, 1964.

Carney, Francis. *The Rise of Democratic Clubs in California.* New York: McGraw-Hill, 1960.

Clark, Thomas D., and Albert D. Kirwan. *The South since Appomattox: A Century of Regional Change.* New York: Oxford University Press, 1967.

Costikyan, Edward N. *Behind Closed Doors.* New York: Harcourt Brace Jovanovich, 1966.

Council of State Governments. *The Book of the States, 1935 [-1975].* Chicago and Lexington, Ky.: Council of State Governments, 1935 [-1975].

Cox, Edward Franklin. *State and National Voting in Federal Elections, 1910-1970.* Hamden, Conn.: Shoe String Press, 1972.

Crew, Robert E., Jr., ed. *State Politics: Readings on Political Behavior.* Belmont, Calif.: Wadsworth Publishing Company, 1968.

Dabney, Virginius. *Virginia: The New Dominion.* New York: Doubleday and Company, 1971.

____. *Dry Messiah: The Life of Bishop Cannon.* New York: Knopf, 1949.

Dallinger, Frederick W. *Nominations for Elective Office in the United States.* Cambridge: Harvard University Press, 1897.

David, Paul T., and Ralph Eisenberg. *Devaluation of the Urban and Suburban Vote.* Charlottesville: Bureau of Public Administration, University of Virginia, 1961.

Duverger, Maurice. *Political Parties: Their Organization and Activity in the Modern State.* New York: John Wiley and Sons, 1954.

Eisenberg, Ralph. *Virginia Votes, 1924-1968.* Charlottesville: Institute of Government, University of Virginia, 1971.

Ewing, Cortez A. M. *Primary Elections in the South: A Study in Uniparty Politics.* Norman: University of Oklahoma Press, 1953.

Eyre, R. John, and Curtis Martin. *The Colorado Preprimary System.* Boulder: Bureau of Governmental Research and Service, University of Colorado, 1967.

Fanning, Clara Elizabeth, ed. *Selected Articles on Direct Primaries.* 4th ed. New York: H. W. Wilson Company, 1918.

Fesler, James W., ed. *The 50 States and Their Local Governments.* New York: Knopf, 1967.

Gooch, Robert Kent. *The Poll Tax in Virginia Suffrage History: A Premature Proposal for Reform (1941).* Charlottesville: Institute of Government, University of Virginia, 1969.

Goodman, William. *The Two-Party System in the United States.* 3d ed. New York: D. Van Nostrand Company, 1964.

Gottmann, Jean. *Virginia at Mid-Century.* New York: Henry Holt, 1955.

Greenstein, Fred I. *The American Party System and the American People.* 2d ed. Englewood Cliffs, N.J.: Prentice-Hall, 1970.

Grimes, Marcene D. *Kansas Primaries.* Lawrence: Governmental Research Center, University of Kansas, 1954.

Harris, Joseph P. *California Politics.* Stanford: Stanford University Press, 1955.

Havard, William C., ed. *The Changing Politics of the South.* Baton Rouge: Louisiana State University Press, 1969.

Hawley, Willis D. *Nonpartisan Elections and the Case for Party Politics.* New York: John Wiley and Sons, 1973.

Heard, Alexander. *A Two-Party South?* Chapel Hill: University of North Carolina Press, 1952.

Heard, Alexander, and Donald S. Strong. *Southern Primaries and Elections, 1920–1949.* University: University of Alabama, 1950.

Hinderaker, Joan. *Party Politics.* New York: Henry Holt and Company, 1956.

Holland, Lynwood Mathis. *The Direct Primary in Georgia.* Urbana: University of Illinois Press, 1949.

Holloway, Harry. *The Politics of the Southern Negro.* New York: Random House, 1969.

Jacob, Herbert, and Kenneth N. Vines, eds. *Politics in the American States.* 2d ed. Boston: Little, Brown, and Company, 1971.

James, Judson L. *American Political Parties in Transition.* New York: Harper and Row, 1974.

Jewell, Malcolm E., and Samuel C. Patterson. *The Legislative Process in the United States.* New York: Random House, 1966.

Jewell, Malcolm E. *Legislative Representation in the Contemporary South.* Durham, N.C.: Duke University Press, 1967.

Jonas, Frank H., ed. *Politics in the American West.* Salt Lake City: University of Utah Press, 1969.

Judah, Charles, and Oliver E. Payne. *New Mexico's Proposed Pre-Primary Designating Convention.* Albuquerque: Department of Government, University of New Mexico, 1950.

Key, V. O., Jr. *Southern Politics in State and Nation.* New York: Knopf, 1949.
——. *American State Politics: An Introduction.* New York: Knopf, 1956.
——. *Politics, Parties, and Pressure Groups.* 5th ed. New York: Thomas Y. Crowell Company, 1964.

Kirby, Jack Temple. *Westmoreland Davis: Virginia Planter-Politician, 1859–1942.* Charlottesville: University Press of Virginia, 1968.

Kirwan, Albert D. *Revolt of the Rednecks.* Lexington: University of Kentucky Press, 1951.

LaFollette, Robert M. *LaFollette's Autobiography.* Madison: University of Wisconsin Press, 1960.

Lewinson, Paul. *Race, Class, and Party.* New York: Oxford University Press, 1932.

Lockard, Duane. *New England State Politics.* Princeton, N.J.: Princeton University Press, 1959.

——. *Connecticut's Challenge Primary: A Study in Legislative Politics.* New York: McGraw-Hill, 1960.

——. *The Politics of State and Local Government.* New York: Macmillan, 1963.

Lovejoy, Allen Fraser. *LaFollette and the Establishment of the Direct Primary in Wisconsin, 1890–1904.* New Haven: Yale University Press, 1941.

McDanel, Ralph Clipman. *The Virginia Constitutional Convention of 1901–1902.* Baltimore: Johns Hopkins Press, 1928.

Merriam, Charles E., and Louise Overacker. *Primary Elections.* Chicago: University of Chicago Press, 1928.

Merriam, Charles E. *Primary Elections: A Study of the History and Tendencies of Primary Election Legislation.* Chicago: University of Chicago Press, 1909.

Michie Company. *Michie's Jurisprudence of Virginia and West Virgina.* 24 vols. Charlottesville, Michie Company, 1949.

Mitau, G. Theodore. *Politics in Minnesota.* 2d ed. rev. Minneapolis: University of Minnesota Press, 1970.

Moger, Allen W. *Virginia: Bourbonism to Byrd, 1870–1930.* Charlottesville: University Press of Virginia, 1968.

Morris, Thomas R. *Virginia's Lieutenant Governors: The Office and the Person.* Charlottesville: Institute of Government, University of Virginia, 1970.

Munger, Frank, ed. *American State Politics: Readings for Comparative Analysis.* New York: Thomas J. Crowell Company, 1966.

——, and Douglas Price, eds. *Readings in Political Parties and Pressure Groups.* New York: Thomas J. Crowell Company, 1964.

National Municipal League. *A Model Direct Primary System.* New York: National Municipal League, 1951.

Nye, Russel B. *Midwestern Progressive Politics.* East Lansing: Michigan State College Press, 1951.

Pollock, James Kerr. *The Direct Primary in Michigan, 1909–1935.* Ann Arbor: University of Michigan Press, 1943.

Pulley, Raymond H. *Old Virginia Restored: An Interpretation of the Progressive Impulse, 1870–1930.* Charlottesville: University Press of Virginia, 1968.

Ranney, Austin. *The Doctrine of Responsible Party Government.* Urbana: University of Illinois Press, 1962.

Ransone, Coleman B., Jr. *The Office of Governor in the United States.* University: University of Alabama Press, 1956.

Sabato, Larry. *Aftermath of Armageddon: An Analysis of the 1973 Virginia Gubernatorial Election.* Charlottesville: Institute of Government, University of Virginia, 1975.

———. *Virginia Notes, 1969–1974.* Charlottesville: Institute of Government, University of Virginia, 1976.

Scammon, Richard M., ed. *America Votes.* Vols. 1–9. New York: Macmillan, 1956–70.

Schattschneider, E. E. *Party Government.* New York: Holt, Rinehart, and Winston, 1942.

Schlesinger, Joseph A. *How They Became Governor: A Study of Comparative State Politics, 1870–1950.* East Lansing: Governmental Research Bureau, Michigan State University, 1957.

Simkins, Francis B. *The Tillman Movement in South Carolina.* Durham, N.C.: Duke University Press, 1926.

Sindler, Allan P. *Political Parties in the United States.* New York: St. Martin's Press, 1966.

Sorauf, Frank J. *Party and Representation: Legislative Politics in Pennsylvania.* New York: Atherton Press, 1963.

———. *Political Parties in the American System.* Boston: Little, Brown, and Company, 1964.

———. *Party Politics in America.* Boston: Little, Brown, and Company, 1968.

Tarrance, Lance, and Walter DeVries. *The Ticket-Splitter: A New Force in American Politics.* Grand Rapids, Mich.: William B. Eerdmans Publishing Company, 1972.

Tayloe Murphy Institute and the Institute of Government, University of Virginia. *The Virginia Constituency: Election District Data, 1970.* Charlottesville: Institute of Government, University of Virginia, 1973.

Thomas Jefferson Center for Political Economy. *Statistical Abstract of Virginia.* Vols. 1 and 2. Charlottesville: University of Virginia, 1966, 1970.

Thumm, Garold W., and Edward G. Janosik. *Parties and the Governmental System.* Englewood Cliffs, N.J.: Prentice-Hall, 1967.

Tindall, George B. *The Emergence of the New South, 1913–1945.* Baton Rouge: Louisiana State University Press, 1967.

Tufte, Edward R. *Data Analysis for Politics and Policy.* Englewood Cliffs, N.J.: Prentice-Hall, 1974.

Wilkinson, J. Harvie, III. *Harry Byrd and the Changing Face of Virginia Politics.* Charlottesville: University Press of Virginia, 1968.

Woodward, C. Vann. *Origins of the New South, 1877–1913.* Baton Rouge: Louisiana State University Press, 1951.

Periodicals

Dowdey, Clifford. "Virginia, 1865–1965: The Story of a Century." *Virginia Record* 87 (1965): 7, 55.

Eisenberg, Ralph. "Virginia Votes for President: Patterns and Prospects." *University of Virginia News Letter* 41 (Sept. 15, 1964): 1–4.

———. "The 1964 Presidential Election in Virginia: A Political Omen?" *University of Virginia News Letter* 41 (April 15, 1965): 29–32.

———. "Gubernatorial Politics in Virginia: The Experience of 1965." *University of Virginia News Letter* 45 (Mar. 15, 1969): 25–28.

———. "1966 Politics in Virginia: The Elections for U.S. Representatives." *University of Virginia News Letter* 43 (June 15, 1967): 37–40.

———. "1966 Politics in Virginia: The Elections for U.S. Senators." *University of Virginia News Letter* 43 (May 15, 1967): 33–36.

———. "The 1968 Election in Virginia: Voting Patterns and Party Competition." *University of Virginia News Letter* 45 (June 15, 1969): 37–40.

———. "1969 Politics in Virginia: The Democratic Party Primary." *University of Virginia News Letter* 46 (Feb. 15, 1970): 21–24.

———. "1969 Politics in Virginia: The General Election." *University of Virginia News Letter* 46 (May 15, 1970): 33–36.

———. "The 1970 U.S. Senate Election in Virginia: Independent Voting and Turnout Patterns." *University of Virginia News Letter* 48 (Oct. 15, 1971): 5–8.

Ford, Henry Jones. "The Direct Primary." *North American Review* 190 (July 1909): 1–14.

Hacker, Andrew. "Does a 'Divisive' Primary Harm a Candidate's Election Chances?" *American Political Science Review* 59 (1965): 105–10.

Holtzmann, Abraham. "The Loyalty Pledge Controversy in the Democratic Party." Case No. 21 in *Cases in Practical Politics.* Eagleton Institute Series, Rutgers University. New York: McGraw-Hill, 1960.

Hughes, Charles Evans. "The Fate of the Direct Primary." *National Municipal Review* 10 (1921): 23–31.

Jewell, Malcolm E. "Party and Primary Competition in Kentucky State Legislative Races." *Kentucky Law Journal* 48 (1960): 517–535.

Kelley, George M. "The Changing Style of Virginia Politics." *University of Virginia News Letter* 45 (Feb. 15, 1969): 21–24.

Kirby, Jack Temple. "The Democratic Organization and Its Challenges 1899–1922." *Virginia Social Science Journal* 1 (1966): 35.

Lockard, Duane. "Connecticut Gets a Primary." *National Municipal Review* 44 (1955): 469.

——. "Connecticut's Challenge Primary: A Study in Legislative Politics." Case No. 7 in *Cases in Practical Politics*. Eagleton Institute Series, Rutgers University. New York: McGraw-Hill, 1960.

Moger, Allen W. "The Origin of the Democratic Machine in Virginia." *Journal of Southern History* 8 (1942): 183–209.

Ogden, Daniel M., Jr. "The Blanket Primary and Party Regularity in Washington." *Pacific Northwest Quarterly* 39 (1948): 33–38.

——. "Washington's Popular Primary." *Research Studies of Washington State College* 19 (1951): 139–61.

Pidgeon, Mary E., ed. "Primary and Convention." *University of Virginia Record, Extension Series*, 10 (Nov. 1925): 1–106.

Porter, Kirk H. "The Deserted Primary in Iowa." *American Political Science Review* 39 (1945): 732–740.

Pulley, Raymond H. "The May Movement of 1899: Irresolute Progressivism in the Old Dominion." *Virginia Magazine of History and Biography* 75 (April 1967): 186–201.

Ranney, Austin. "The Representativeness of Primary Electorates." *Midwest Journal of Political Science* 12 (1968): 224–238.

——, and Leon D. Epstein. "The Two Electorates: Voters and Non-Voters in a Wisconsin Primary." *Journal of Politics* 28 (1966): 598–616.

Sabato, Larry. "Virginia's Urban Areas: Flexing Political Muscles." *Virginia Town and City* 9 (Sept. 1974): 73–78.

——. "Virginia Congressional Elections in 1974: The Year of the Democrats." *University of Virginia News Letter* 51 (April 15, 1975): 29–32.

Sindler, Allan P. "Bifactional Rivalry as an Alternative to Two-Party Competition in Louisiana." *American Political Science Review* 49 (1955): 641–662.

Standing, William H., and James A. Robinson. "Inter-Party Competition and Primary Contesting: The Case of Indiana." *American Political Science Review* 52 (1958): 1066–1077.

Turner, Julius. "Primary Elections as the Alternative to Party Competition in 'Safe' Districts." *Journal of Politics* 15 (1953): 197–210.

Weeks, O. Douglas. "The Texas Direct Primary System." *Southwestern Social Science Quarterly* 13 (1932): 95–120.

——. "The White Primary." *Mississippi Law Journal* 8 (Dec. 1935): 135–53.

Williams, Murat W. "Virginia Politics: Winds of Change." *Virginia Quarterly Review* 42 (1966): 177.

——. "Origins of the Direct Primary." *National Municipal Review* 24 (1935): 222–23.

Newspapers

Articles appearing in the following newspapers were quoted or consulted:

Richmond Times
Richmond Dispatch
Richmond Times-Dispatch
Richmond News Leader
Richmond Mercury
Roanoke Times
Norfolk *Virginian*
Norfolk *Virginian-Pilot*
Norfolk *Ledger-Star*
Fredericksburg *Free-Lance Star*
Charlottesville *Daily Progress*
Winchester *Evening Star*
Washington Post
Washington *Evening Star*
Lynchburg *News*

Manuscripts

Bear, James A., Jr. "Thomas Staples Martin—A Study in Virginia Politics, 1883–1896." M.A. thesis, University of Virginia, 1952.

Doss, Richard B. "John Warwick Daniel: A Study in the Virginia Democracy." Ph.D. dissertation, University of Virginia, 1955.

Ferrell, Henry Clifton, Jr. "Claude A. Swanson of Virginia." Ph.D. dissertation, University of Virginia, 1964.

Larsen, William Edward. "Governor Andrew Jackson Montague of Virginia, 1862–1937: The Making of a Southern Progressive." Ph.D. dissertation, University of Virginia, 1961.

Latimer, James. "Virginia Politics, 1950–1960." Manuscript by the chief political reporter for the Richmond *Times-Dispatch*. Richmond, 1961.

Moore, Lois Grier. "William Alexander Anderson, Attorney General of Virginia, 1902–1910." M.A. thesis, University of Virginia, 1959.

Poindexter, Harry Edward. "From Copy Desk to Congress: The Pre-Congressional Career of Carter Glass." Ph.D. dissertation, University of Virginia, 1966.

Rankin, Robert A. "Black Power Politics: The Crusade for Voters in Richmond, Virginia." M.A. thesis, University of Virginia, 1974.

Shibley, Ronald E. "Election Laws and Electoral Practices in Virginia, 1867–1902: An Administrative and Political History." Ph.D. dissertation, University of Virginia, 1972.

Wolfe, Jonathan J. "The Gubernatorial Election of 1941." M.A. thesis, University of Virginia, 1968.

Index